A

THE MISSING PEACE

THE ROLE OF RELIGION IN THE **ARAB-ISRAELI** CONFLICT

© 2015 - Omer Salem / Averroës Books
All rights reserved.

No part of this book may be used or reproduced by any means, graphic, electronic, or mechanical, including photocopying, recording, taping or by any information storage retrieval system without the written permission of the author /publisher except in the case of brief quotations embodied in critical articles and reviews.

Contact Professor Salem at **omer.salem@aya.yale.edu**

Averroës Books is an imprint of the **Ibn Rushd Institute**
ibnrushd.org

ISBN: 978-0-9965924-3-7 - *softcover*
978-0-9965924-1-3 - *hardcover*
978-0-9965924-2-0 - *e-book*

PUBLISHED IN THE UNITED STATES OF AMERICA

BOOK DESIGN
www.timmyroland.com

COVER IMAGE
www.shutterstock.com

*In the hopes of building a better world for our children,
I dedicate this book to my children*

**Sarah, Dahlia, Yousuf, Alia, Hamid,
Sorya, and Yasmeen**

*whose support and encouragement enriched
the quest that led me here.*

THE MISSING PEACE
THE ROLE OF RELIGION IN THE **ARAB-ISRAELI** CONFLICT

"O mankind! We created you from a single (pair) of a male and a female, and made you into nations and tribes, that ye may know each other. Verily the most honored of you in the sight of Allah is the person who is the most virtuous of you."

Qur'an 49:13

THE MISSING PEACE
THE ROLE OF RELIGION IN THE **ARAB-ISRAELI** CONFLICT

Endorsements

"I bless the author of this book, whose concern is that all those who fear G-d serve Him together, in the way that G-d desires."

    Rav Yoel Schwartz,
    Yeshivat Dvar Yerushalayim

" . . . you have presented a different way of regarding the Arab-Israeli conflict from a moral and human point of view. I liked in particular your proposal for inviting the Arab Jews back to their homes in the Arab world."

    Dr. Ghada Karmi, Palestinian Native of Jerusalem
    Professor of Arab and Islamic Studies, Exeter University, Devon, UK

"I hope this will become the majority voice among the followers of the three Abrahamic religions."

    Dr. Yaser M. Najjar, Dean of Graduate Studies
    Farmington State University, Farmington, Massachusetts, USA

"I just want to bless you for your warm heart that seeks to build a bridge between Arabs and Jews. I encourage you to keep up your efforts."

    Canon Brian Cox, Episcopal Priest
    International Center for Religion and Diplomacy
    Washington, District of Columbia, USA

"Incredible and has made me think in new ways."

Rabbi Ephraim Gabbai
Sixteenth Street Synagogue, New York City, New York, USA

"Thank you for your lifetime of scholarship that has led to your ability to write such significant contribution to the challenges you address."

Bishop Gordon Scruton
Episcopal Church, Springfield, Massachusetts, USA

"Omer, thank you for the book, it is very inspiring."

Rabbi Patricia Karlin-Neumann
Senior Associate Dean for Religious Life
Stanford University, Palo Alto, California, USA

"You are mastering the method we think will work best: using the orthodox religious text to support the belief that God wants all humans to speak their truth honestly and at the same time to be patient with each other's conflicting religious beliefs - not forcing agreement today."

Dr. Charles Randal Paul Founder and President
Foundation for Religious Diplomacy New York, New York, USA

"I found the thesis fascinating and I must say, I was moved by the proposal of inviting Jews to live in Arab lands."

Dr. Mohammad Khalil
Professor of Middle Eastern Studies
Michigan State University, Lansing, Michigan, USA

"Indeed, [the paper] does represent a unique and engaging position on the middle-east peace process."

Peter Salovey, Provost
Yale University, New Haven, Connecticut, USA

ENDORSEMENTS

"Omer Salem's provocative and intelligent work is an invitation to all of us to find within our traditions resources for respect and coexistence . . . These are potentially world-changing ideas. Imagine in a world in which, as Omer Salem says "we compete in righteousness." Who would not want to live in such a world?"

        Lee Weissman, Orthodox Jew and Peace Activist
        Irvine, Califorina, USA

"You bring an understanding of Arab history that's not generally known in the West. You propose specific actions that Arab governments can implement that would benefit Jews without jeopardizing Arab security [and] You emphasize the importance of a religious solution in the Middle East, a topic that is often minimized by Western diplomacy."

        Kenneth Godshall, Pastor
        Central Presbyterian Church
        Princeton, Kentucky, USA

"I think the basic principles that you are espousing are the correct principles that we will have to follow if we are to make progress on these very difficult matters."

        Bishop Richard Jacobsen, Stake President of LDS Church
        Menlo Park, California, USA

"This is great! I thoroughly enjoyed reading it and am very encouraged and moved by your ideas...certainly to break the deadlock someone has to take the first step and in a sense be willing to risk suffering injustice. Also confessing sin, repenting and making restitution is also central to Christian practice."

        Philip McCollum Department of Sociology
        School of Humanities and Social Sciences
        Exeter University, Devon, UK

" . . . you have correctly noted the significance of views related to blessings and curses related to those who help Israel. Perhaps even more important is your recognition of dispensationalist views of biblical prophecy to how Israel and "Palestine" are viewed."

John W. Morehead
Evangelical Christian Foundation for Religious Diplomacy
Salt Lake City, Utah, USA

"... Muslims, especially Arabs, now and in the past, have been , and still are, responsible and thus accountable for the pathetic situation of Jewish and non-Jewish people of the Holy Land... It is, indeed, commendable and necessary to remind ourselves and everyone else to be compassionate and merciful, as has been ordered by Allah(SWT)."

Ali Shakibai, MD
Tehran University of Medical Sciences, Faculty of Medicine,
Tehran, Iran

"It is EXCELLENT. If Jews, Christians and Muslims lived their religion and gave others the same right and respect the world would be at peace."

Boyd Smith, Stake President
The Church of Jesus Christ for Later Day Saints
Palo Alto, California, USA

"Omer Salem offers a timely and feasible path to peace - he proves that for the faithful Jew and the faithful Muslim there is no other way but that of peace."

James David Audlin, Author, Scholar, Translator
Pasco Ancho, Panama

ENDORSEMENTS

"It is an excellently written book. I am excited that it places, what I feel, proper emphasis on the role of religion in the region. The appeal to Islamic Moral Values is a very powerful argument."

Benjamin Abrahamson
Orthodox Hasidic Jew, Judge in Israeli Religious Courts
Mea Shearim, Jerusalem, State of Israel

THE
MISSING PEACE
THE ROLE OF RELIGION IN THE **ARAB-ISRAELI** CONFLICT

Contents

Endorsements . . . . *i*
Acknowledgements . . . . *xi*
Preface . . . . *xiii*
Introduction
   The Role of Religion in the Middle East: Arab Awakening . . 1

Section I
Basic Framework for Conciliation
   The World is More Religious 15
   Diversity 16
   The Seven Noachide Laws 18
   Commonalities 20
   Uniqueness of Each revelations 23
   Religion and Government 24
   Dignitism and Peace 25
   The Jews and the Land 31
   The Oppressed of the Land: Palestinian Refugees 37
   The Palestinian Refugees 41
   Replace PLO with HLCO 45
   The Scattered in the Land: Jewish refugees 47
   Jewish Security vs Arab Dignity 52
   Jews in Arab Lands 53
   Holy Land 61
   Jerusalem and Mecca 63
   Haram Sharif (The Temple Mount) 64

Section II
The Top Ten Objections to Repatriation
    1. Jewish and Arab Enmity 71
    2. Jews as Neighbors 74

3. Can Jews and Christians Accept Muslims? 75
4. The Return of all Refugees 76
5. Who May Finance Repatriation 77
6. The Claim that Zionism Does not Support Peace . . . 78
7. Aggression Rewarded 79
8. Some Jews May Refuse Repatriation 80
9. Concessions with Nothing in Return 81
10. Might Arabs be Getting Cheated? 82

Selected Photographs
From the author's peacemaking activities 86

Section III
Striving for Virtue, Dignitism, Scripture
Tolerance and Respect 103
The Purpose of the Scripture 107
Coexistence 114
Arabrahamic Traditions are helpful Rivals 115
Conclusion 121
Summary
Points to Solve the Conflict 125
Epilogue 131
Resources 133
Definition of Terms 137
Exhibits
One: The Bible 143
Two: The Qur'an 149
Three: Ethnic Cleansing 152
Four: Land Swap 1 153
Five: Land Swap 2 154
Six: Twelve Tribes of Israel 155
Bibliography 157
Letters of Support
Arabic 160
English 166
Index 173
About the author 179

THE ROLE OF RELIGION IN THE **ARAB-ISRAELI** CONFLICT

OMER **SALEM**

NEW HAVEN, CONNECTICUT

THE MISSING PEACE
THE ROLE OF RELIGION IN THE **ARAB-ISRAELI** CONFLICT

Acknowledgements

II wish to thank the people whose names appear below for their part in inspiring me to write and edit this book. While it is unlikely that any participant would claim to be in total agreement with the final book that ultimately emerged, all will find some reflection of their respective contributions. Those who offered insights, suggestions, and commentary include the following:

Bishop Boyd Smith
Bishop Gordon Scruton
Dr. Charles Randall Paul
Dr. Ghada Karmi
Dr. Mohamed H. Khalil
Imam Dr. Abdul Aziz Sachedina
Imam Dr. Ekrema Sabri
Imam Dr. Mohamed Al-Fiqui
Imam Dr. Omar Shahin
Imam Dr. Tahir Kukiqi
Imam Wathiq Al-Ubaidi
Monsignor Steven Otellini

Professor Harold Attridge
Rabbi Ari Cartun
Rabbi Dr. Burton Visotzky
Rabbi Dr. Reuven Firestone
Rabbi Ephraim Gabi
Rabbi Herbert Brockman
Rabbi Sheldon Lewis
Reverend Dr. Joseph Cumming
Reverend Edward Rawel
Reverend James David Audlin
Reverend Peter Drekmeier

To you the reader, we are grateful for your willingness to explore the ideas shared in this book with an open mind. In our world today the level of violence based on misquoting and misunderstanding religious text suggests that peacemakers need to double their efforts towards reconciliation. The simmering fires of religious demagoguery make it almost impossible to have peace between adherents of the Abrahamic traditions. This work attempts to pour water on such hot issues.

THE MISSING PEACE

THE ROLE OF RELIGION IN THE **ARAB-ISRAELI** CONFLICT

Preface

Egypt in the sixties and seventies for the Salem family was a balance between keeping Islamic tradition at home and attending the secular system of public schools, which would provide us with the best of opportunities, and form us into what my parents considered model Muslims. Both traditional Islamic practice and a breadth of scholarship were to be revered, in line with the great Islamic thinkers that always inspired us like Imam Mohamed Abdu and M. Rashid Reda.[1]

I was first exposed to other cultures and peoples when I traveled on foot and auto-stop on a forty-day journey to Europe in the summer of 1974. I was only fourteen at the time, but that journey taught me many valuable lessons, including the importance of being independent, self-sufficient, relating to others and understanding different cultures and people. That journey to Europe was followed by three more journeys to Europe and the Middle East for the following three summers, before our family emigrated and settled in California in the late seventies.

Having lived in three different countries on three different continents, I have had no choice but to consider many different points of view, not only in my own acclimation from Egyptian to American culture, and then to Indian culture and back to American, but in my desire to understand the Middle East conflict at its root. Many of my relatives and friends still reside in Egypt. Therefore, my interest in solving the conflict is both on an ideological and personal level.

My personal and global journey included study at Berkeley and Stanford universities, after which I established myself in a real estate investment business. I then embarked on a trek to the Indian subcontinent, where I spent some time with the pacifist Muslim

Tablighi Jamaat movement and experienced again a taste of wandering, joined with outreach to other Muslims and simplicity in living. My passion for solving the conflicts in the Middle East led me to pursue a master's degree at Yale Divinity School, then a PhD, supervised and defended at Al-Azhar University, Cairo, Egypt.

Once a person sees so many points of view, from so many strata of society and cultures, one is no longer able to come up with glib answers; indeed, the reader will see a variety of views reflected here, as I have tried to truly understand each party to the conflict. I thus cannot guarantee that you will be comfortable with all I say. I just ask that you see this through until the end, noting where I validate what you are familiar with, and accommodating the ideas that may be new. I am convinced that solutions are at hand via the shared traditions that Islam and Judaism hold to, requiring a little patience to navigate them through our varied perspectives.

---

1 - Both are Egyptian Muslim jurists, religious scholars and reformers

INTRODUCTION

The Role of Religion in the Arab Israeli Conflict
Adapted from my speech to the United States Congress
September 2012

Religion plays an important role in the lives and daily practices of most people in the Middle East. Ninety-nine percent of the inhabitants of the Middle East are part of an Abrahamic faith. The remaining one percent may be atheists or members of other religions. Thus, the vast majority trace their common origin to the Patriarch Abraham (d. 1650 BCE). About two percent of the inhabitants of the Middle East trace the origin of their faith to the Prophet Abraham through his son Isaac—they call their faith and that of Abraham "Judaism". Another six percent of the inhabitants of the Middle East trace their faith to the Prophet Abraham through his son Isaac—they call their faith and that of Abraham "Christianity".

The majority of the inhabitants of the Middle East, about ninety-two percent, trace the origin of their faith to the Prophet Abraham through his son Ishmael—they call their faith and that of Abraham "Islam". The term "Islam" bears two connotations—in a broader sense, it means anyone who submits to the One God; in this vein, the Holy Qur'an defines Islam as the restored religion of Abraham. "Islam" is widely known more specifically as the religion of the

1

followers of the Prophet Muhammad. Muslims regard Abraham as a prophet and patriarch, the archetype of the perfect Muslim, and the revered reformer of the Kaaba in Mecca. While ninety-two percent of Arabs are Muslims, only eighteen percent of Muslims are Arabs.

I realize that Arabs are not the only cultural group involved in the conflict over Israel. Iranians and others are also important factors in the problem. Specifically, Shi'ite interpretations of Islamic sacred texts sometimes differ from Sunni views, and those Shi'a interpretations surely are part of the Missing Peace. However, as a Sunni I have studied mainly with Arab Sunni scholars and the title of this book reflects my focus on Arabian religious culture.

The centrality of religion in the Middle East was boldly made clear in 2011, when the world witnessed a spate of grassroots uprisings across the Arab world which became known as the "Arab Spring". The members of the Arab population who took part in these uprisings utilized the moral values of religion as a unifying and driving force to get rid of despotic, corrupt regimes. Indeed, crowds in Tahrir Square, Egypt and elsewhere expressed their religious devotion by kneeling and prostrating themselves while being attacked by security forces.

I was heartbroken to witness such expressions of frustration and violence in my homeland, and terribly worried about friends and family who still reside in Egypt. Tahrir square is a short distance away from where I grew up. Imagine a place you love going up in flames; you would do anything you could to douse the fires. I believe that one thing that will help douse such flames of conflict is an awareness of Islamic moral values – and these values are not totally foreign to Judaism or to the West, which we shall see herein.

The Arab Awakening took everyone, including Arabs, by surprise. No one in the west, nor the now-deposed leaders in the Middle East, predicted those revolutions, and there is only speculation about where they might go. As Thomas Friedman quipped, "If you did not see it coming, what makes you think you know where it is going?"[1]

All four countries that had regime changes (Egypt, Libya, Tunisia and Yemen) shared four factors: aging autocratic rulers, high levels of corruption and nepotism, lack of dignity for ordinary citizens, and police brutality.

Because these failed regimes were supported and, on occasion, praised by various American administrations, the reputation of the United States in the Middle East stands to suffer for some time to come. For America to be viewed by Arabs and Muslims as the endorsers of corrupt, dictatorial regimes should provoke some serious soul searching in the United States in its claims to be a beacon of democracy while not always holding to those values abroad. American President Barack Obama tried to undo some of this damage in his 2009 historic speech in Cairo:

> "All people yearn for certain things: the ability to speak your mind and have a say in how you are governed; confidence in the rule of law and the equal administration of justice; government that is transparent and does not steal from the people and the freedom to live as you choose."[2]

Revolutionaries in the recent Arab Awakening drew on their people's Islamic values and traditions to fuel the uprisings that toppled their regimes. While these revolutionaries used technology and social media, it was the people's reliance on religious moral values, as delineated in a book entitled *La Morale Du Coran, The Revolution Succeeded*,[3] that fueled the success of the revolutions. This is reflected in the fact that all autocratic regime changes in those countries involved replacing existing regimes by religiously leaning parties, parliaments, and or governments.

That Islamic moral values formed the basis for the Arab awakening and uprisings shows the deep connection that Arab Muslims in the Middle East have to their religion. Thus, the Islamic tradition and the Holy Qur'an are the ideal source of peacemaking efforts; any attempts to rely on UN charters, international law, the constitutions of the various Arab states, or any other document will likely fail. This is because it is the Holy Qur'an that Middle Eastern Arab Muslims revere as the guiding force of their lives. In their view, it is the ultimate source of wisdom that trumps all else. There is simply no other document that can hope to compete in holding the attention and respect of Arab Muslims, whether intended as guidance for one's personal, communal, or even national life. This is what I presented to the United States Senate, the Israeli Knesset, the Egyptian Parliament and at my dissertations at both Yale and Al-Azhar universities, with enthusiastic feedback in response.

Many in the west are generally unaccustomed to using religion as a base for peacemaking. However, western leaders can see the reverence that Muslims have for scripture as a wonderful opportunity to hold them accountable to the very values in which they take pride and feel ownership for. When Islamic values are used in peacemaking, Arab Muslims will feel accountable, empowered, responsible for and in control of their national destiny. Then we will see fewer voices from the Arab world claiming that they are being manipulated, or as is often claimed, "colonized". Accusations of conspiracies against Muslims will fade as they take the reins with the scripture and tradition that they hold dear. And, by the way, scripture is open to all, Muslim and non-Muslim alike. Anyone can study the Qur'an and Hadith and hold Muslims accountable to any and all claims that they make based upon scripture.

Muslims respect the holy Qur'an and pious Jews respect the Torah, and both sets of scriptures can be used harmoniously in peace negotiations, giving the peoples of the region a feeling of ownership in that what is delineating any peace treaty springs from their own holy writ. Moreover, Islamic values are consistent with the teachings of the Bible, and even with western political science as revitalized by Thomas Luber Erastus (sixteenth century Switzerland).

Our shared Biblical values include belief in one God, respect of the creation vis-a-vis prohibitions against cruelty to animals, the importance of the family unit, prohibitions against murder and theft, guarding the tongue, prohibitions against gossip, bigotry and prejudice, commandments regarding prayer, charity, fasting, and the establishment of a justice system. In this last vein, appointing credible and God-fearing judges recognized by both sides is key to achieving inter-religious peace in the Holy Land.

What Islam shares with even modern political science has been largely ignored in recent history: Thomas Luber Erastus actually proposed that the ancient Hebrew Commonwealth be utilized as a paradigm for modern political theory. Erastus's followers included the founders of the English Parliament and the founding fathers of the United States of America. Thus, the similarities between the Qur'an and the Bible have a direct bearing on Islam's similarities with modern political theory.[4] We are not so foreign to each other.

The Arab-Israeli conflict and the Arab Spring

Despite the regime changes in the wake of the Arab Spring, the Arab world still views Israel as a common enemy. They can always find media reports that justify their position that Israel is viewed as a colonial aggressor and occupier, to be uprooted by force if necessary. Therefore, it is important to find a solution for this nagging conflict before more innocent blood from both sides is spilled.

For many years, the Arab-Israeli conflict has seemed intractable.[5] Its solution has eluded most world and regional political leaders on all sides. In the words of one scholar, this conflict is becoming more and more like the Greek classic legend of Phrygian Gordium, the "Gordian Knot."[6] The legend is associated with Alexander the Great and is often used as a metaphor for an intractable problem solved by "thinking outside the box".

Herein, an "out of the box" solution is discussed—surprisingly simple, elegant and supported by wise and educated people on both sides of the conflict: **the Arab Israeli conflict is intractable because some of the participants, many observers and would-be peace makers have focused primarily on political and economic solutions and have sidelined or marginalized the elephant in the room—religion.**

Because Islam does not separate between church and state, the religion of Islam amounts to political Islam—and this is not completely foreign to the West.[7]

Indeed, John Selden, seventeenth century political theorist, relied heavily upon Biblical concepts concerning nationhood in international relations.[8]

The Arab Awakening showed unequivocally that "political Islam is poised to dominate the new world order."[9] As professor John Louis Esposito, states, "Political Islam is a set of ideologies holding that

Islam is as much a political ideology as a religion".[10] Anticipating that Islam would dominate world politics, Professor Harry Attridge, Dean of Yale Divinity School, indicates that relations between Islam and the west "are critical to the fate of the planet"[11]—and the Arab-Israeli conflict lies at the heart of these relations. President Obama's National Security Advisor, General James Jones, put it starkly when he said the Palestinian-Israeli conflict is the "epicenter" of many problems. It ripples around the globe, and solving it would help the United Sates address other challenges. Therefore, if there was one problem to solve in the world, this would be it.[12]

Some might argue that the Arab-Israeli conflict is not a central problem, but a convenient way for MENA political leaders to draw attention away from other problems that plague the Muslim and Arab world.[13] These include slavery in Mauritania; massacres of Christians in Algeria, Egypt Iraq and Syria, the rise of Al-Qaeda in Libya, the migrant worker (kafeel) system in Kingdom of Saudi Arabia ("KSA") , and weapons of mass destruction aspirations in Iran.[14]

Central to world politics or not, the Arab-Israeli conflict is important to solve, and has indeed been intractable because political leaders do not openly address its religious aspects.

Some proposed solutions have been in the economic sphere. Many economic plans have been introduced to end the conflict, including annual aid from the United States to Egypt and Israel, and the promise of decreased defense spending in MENA states.[15] Yet, economic benefits alone will not solve the conflict—a religious solution must be contemplated.

My focus herein is on intellectual frameworks for conciliation between Muslims and Jews, the main objections that some Muslim leaders have against peace with Israel, how to resolve those objections, and, finally, some workable solutions.

We have an ancient biblical story being played out in the Holy Land. There are multiple biblical claims to this contested area, with each group claiming to be the people described in the Bible. Both the Arabs and the Jews view themselves as the legitimate heirs to the prophet and patriarch Abraham. The Jews clearly have a distinction based on the writings of the Bible and Qur'an. Arabs have lived in these lands as long as the Jews have, and also make a claim to the land via their residency therein and descent from Abraham. Although the Philistines are mentioned by name in the Hebrew Bible and by reference in the Qur'an, these scriptures state that God bequeathed the Holy Land to the Children of Abraham in an eternal covenant.

In my view, the struggle is not between the Bible and the Qur'an, for both scriptures complement each other. The struggle is between those who claim to interpret the Bible and Qur'an. We will see herein the inherent harmony between our scriptures and consequent hope for reconciliation. It is my hope that the reader will see herein a new path forward in peace-building for all people of the region.

A note on semantics

Semantics can be a stumbling block, so I would like to clarify the terms often used and then move ahead to better terminology—terminology that will speak to both sides.

Biblical and Qur'anic sources are remarkably similar regarding the relationship of the Jewish people to the Holy Land. What goes wrong is when these quotes are taken out of context for political ends. Herein I will familiarize you with our scriptural sources, discuss how these sources were mistakenly used, and how we can understand our scriptures to bring lasting peace between our peoples.

The Bible refers to the Holy Land with the following terms: the land of Canaan, the land of the Philistines, the Land of Israel, and the Holy Land. Each of these terms is loaded with meaning. The Qur'an uses the term Holy Land, the Blessed Land, the Land of Aqsa Mosque—here we see that both books agree on the term "Holy Land", and this is the term I personally favor.

First, where does the term "Palestine" come from? The land of the Philistines ("Palestine") is a term mentioned in many places in the Hebrew Bible including the book of Genesis (21:34): "And Abraham stayed in the land of the Philistines for a long time." The Philistines saw the establishment of the kingdom of Israel (1030 to 960 BCE). When the Romans destroyed the second Temple in 70 CE, bringing an end to the second Jewish commonwealth, the Romans renamed the Holy Land "Palestine", in part to insult the Jews who had warred with the Philistines. This term then became the common term to refer to this land.

Second, while the term Israel is first mentioned in the book of Genesis, the term "Land of Israel" is first mentioned in First Samuel 13:19: "Not a blacksmith could be found in the whole land of Israel, because the Philistines had said, "Otherwise the Hebrews will make swords or spears!"

Jews feel that they have returned to the land of Israel which was promised to them by God. Depending how you look at it, in 1948 the state of Israel was restored (according to the Jewish people) or taken by force (according to the Arab people).

In my opinion, the Palestinian Arabs are struggling to defend what they refer to as the Land of the Philistines—a term which existed more than three millennia ago, referring to a people who no longer exist. At the same time, the Jews are struggling to have peace with their neighbors after returning to what they call the Land of Israel. Both sides think they have achieved some gains in their struggle over the land, but in fact those gains are only imaginary. Why? Because the Jews failed to find a peace partner or live in peace in the Land of Israel, while the Palestinians failed to have a viable state they can call home and live with dignity in the Land of Palestine. Each side blames the other side for its failure.

I herein propose that the parties have not addressed essential issues in striving for peace. Peace has to be grounded in our respective holy books. While the name Palestine is distasteful to many Jews because of historical enmity, the name Israel is not appreciated by many Arabs because of modern enmity. Thus I suggest the utilization of the term "Holy Land", grounded in both the Bible and Qur'an, to help bring both parties closer to an agreement.

We will see that this small semantic step, based upon a common language we already share, is only the beginning in paving the way towards lasting peace.

At the conclusion of this book I suggest two political strategies for Arab-Israeli peace that are designed to be compatible with Muslim and Jewish religious traditions. I aim to provoke something new: a deeply honest, face-to-face conversation within and between the religious communities that have a theological and practical stake in the economy, governance, and security of the Holy Land about the pros and cons of these and alternative strategies. This is the most efficient way to at least try to create something new together.

The Christians, Jews and Muslims (Shi'a and Sunni) all have scriptures and commentaries about 'how the world will end' or 'the second coming' or 'the apocalypse.' It is very important to understand that if you believe the world has to end by violence, then you will presume—ultimately, all efforts for peace will fail. The deck is stacked against peace, so to speak. In a self-fulfilling prophecy, believers presume that they cannot expect their enemies to change and that they should 'help God' end the world or bring the Final Hour or Second Coming by eliminating their evil enemies violently. The key to this problem is that NO story ends the world with a peaceful conversion of everyone from one faith to another. Just like Jesus Christ—the perfect Lamb of God in Christianity—life ended violently, so the world will end violently. Peace is NOT in the prophesy, so presumably it cannot happen.

The Jews read in Zechariah 14 and Daniel about final wars and the Messiah crushing the Jews' rivals. In the Revelation of Saint John, the end of the world is prophesied as a final war between the angels of God and the evil people on Earth—usually interpreted as those who do not consider Jesus Christ to be Lord and Savior. For the Sunni in the Hadith narrated by Bukhari, Allah will violently punish the wicked or have righteous people fight the wicked people to bring peace and unity to the earth. For the Shi'a, the end is a little different. The Mahdi and Jesus come to end the world and set things in order. At the end good will overcome evil.

The key to this problem is that NO story ends the world with a peaceful conversion of everyone to unity. However, it is by forceful divine intervention—not human action ultimately—that things are put in order. But humans by their peaceful behavior can limit the extent of violent conflict and divine force required at the end time.[16] The stories all point to the triumph of good over evil. This triumph is a common theme in each scripture and can be used and implemented today in our lives without the need for destruction and bloodshed to make it happen. In fact, the Bible and the Qur'an agree on a peaceful—not violent—end of the world as follows: Isaiah 2:2-4 "In the last days the mountain of the LORD's temple will be established as the highest of the mountains; it will be exalted above the hills, and all nations will stream to it. 3 - Many peoples will come and say, "Come, let us go up to the mountain of the LORD, to the temple of the God of Jacob. He will teach us his ways so that we may walk in his paths." The law will go out from Zion, the word of the LORD from Jerusalem. 4 - He will judge between the nations and will settle disputes for many peoples. They will beat their swords into plowshares and their spears into pruning hooks. Nations will not take up sword against nation, *nor will they train for war anymore.*"

Luke 1:78-79 "because of the tender mercy of our God, by which the rising sun will come to us from heaven 79 - to shine on those living in darkness and in the shadow of death, *to guide our feet into the path of peace.*"

Qur'an 24:55 "Allah has promised, to those among you who believe and work righteous deeds, that He will, of a surety, grant them in the land, inheritance of power, as He granted it to those before them; that He will establish in authority their religion—the one that He has chosen for them—and that Allah will change their state, from the fear in which they lived, to one of *security and peace.*

In order to have peace in the Holy Land, one has to start with a vision of what that peace would look like, and find precedence in history and scripture to aid, sustain, maintain and support such a vision. I am persuaded by my reading of scripture, by my listening to the earnest voices on all sides, and by the whispering of my conscience that the divine purpose for the world moves us at this hour to engage in good faith exploration with our religious and political critics and rivals.[17]

INTRODUCTION

---

1 - Thomas Friedman, American journalist, author and three time winner of the Pulitzer Prize writes for New York Times "Watching Elephants Fly," *The New York Times,* January 7, 2012.
2 - Lisa Anderson, Demystifying the Arab Spring, Foreign Affairs, May 2011. P4
3 - Mohamed Abdullah Daraz, Le Morale Du Coran (Paris: Rissalla, 1951), translated to English under the title: A. M. Daraz, Introduction to the Quran, (London: I.B. Tauris, 2000), and translated to Arabic under the title: A.S. Shahin, The constitution of Morales in the Quran
4 - See Exhibits 1 and 2 for the terms: Israel, Palestine and Jerusalem in the Bible and the Quran.
5 - The conflict became intractable to the extent that, at Yale University, April 17, 2012, Dr. Abdel Dayem Nosair, a senior adviser to Al Azhar University Grand Imam, said in response to a question about how to solve the conflict, "I do not know of a solution to this conflict; if you have a solution let me know."
6 - According to Merriam-Webster: an intricate problem; especially: a problem insoluble in its own terms—often used in the phrase cut the Gordian knot.
7 - In the west, it has been the most part forgotten that Thomas Luber Erastus, the father of modern western political theory, was actually inspired by the religious model of the ancient Hebrew commonwealth – so a fusion of religion and state need not be of concern to those in the west, once they rediscover the religious roots of what appears to be totally secular western governments.
8 - John Selden and the International Political System, Abraham Berkowitz, Jewish Political Studies Review, 6: 1-2 Spring 1994
9 - Peter Beaumont, Author of *"The Secret Life of War: Journeys through Modern Conflict",* "Political Islam poised to dominate the new world bequeathed by Arab spring", Foreign Affairs Magazine, December 3, 2011.
10 - John L. Esposito, professor of International Affairs and Islamic Studies and the director of the Prince Alwaleed Bin Talal Center for Muslim-Christian Understanding at Georgetown University and John O. Voll, *Islam and Democracy,* (oxford: Oxford University Press, 1996), p 232.
11 - Harold Attridge, Spectrum Magazine, Yale Divinity School, winter 2012, page 28.
12 - General James Jones' speech on October 27, 2009, at the J street conference "this is the epicenter" (vimeo.com/7302509).
13 - MENA region refers to Middle East and North African countries.
14 - The *Kafeel* system: a restrictive system of holding a foreign employee-passport, banning him or her from traveling within the Kingdom on his or her own and restricting the freedom of transfer of his or her sponsorship.
15 - Defense spending accounts for 6% to 11% of the GDP of MENA countries. The World Fact Book, Central Intelligence Agency. Military Expenditure
16 - This section of the chapter was substantially influenced by the thoughts of Dr. Charles R. Paul, founder of the Foundation of Religious Diplomacy, Salt Lake City, UT.
17 - http//ibnrushd.org/uploads/Omer_Washington_Speech15.pdf

THE MISSING PEACE
THE ROLE OF RELIGION IN THE **ARAB-ISRAELI** CONFLICT

section one

Basic Framework
FOR CONCILIATION

THE MISSING PEACE
THE ROLE OF RELIGION IN THE ARAB-ISRAELI CONFLICT

THE WORLD
IS MORE RELIGIOUS

Diversity, Noachide Covenant, Commonalities, Dignitism
Adapted from my speech to the Israeli Knesset
July 2012

In his book *The Desecularization of the World*, Peter Burger of Boston University debunks an important assumption: "the assumption that we live in a secularized world is false. The world today . . . is as furiously religious as it ever was."[1]

Among Christians, Evangelicals and Pentecostals are the two segments with substantial increase in adherents. Among Jews, it is the Orthodox and its Hasidic subset which are growing.[2] Among Muslims, the Salafi and Tablighi movements are growing. The Holy Book of Islam, the Qur'an, is the most studied, most memorized, and the most respected religious book in the world today, far surpassing interest in the Holy Bible.[3]

The given names "Mohammed" or "Ahmed" are the most common first names for a male in the world.[4]

Therefore, because the world is more religious than secular, and because religion will continue to dominate world politics, especially in the Middle East, religious solutions must be found before addressing political and economic issues. Resolution to conflicts must be based on religious moral values - Islamic values, stemming from exegesis of the Holy Qur'an and Hadith, which have their equivalent in the Bible and even concepts in western political science.[5]

Religion is One, Religious Expression is Diverse

The most potent argument to present to radical Muslim religious leaders is that according to the Qur'an, God is one and *Deen* (basic universal religion) is one, but, *Shari'a* (covenant), is diverse.[6] This is a key distinction to make, as even some scholars tend to confuse the terms "religion" and "covenant". It is important to recognize the difference between *Deen* and *Shari'a*. While all three Abrahamic faiths—Islam, Christianity and Judaism—share the same God and the same *Deen*, they all have different covenants—*Shari'a*—with God.

Deen may be viewed as a diamond. The adherents of any faith tradition should see their own tradition as a diamond. A diamond has four independent criteria: cut, color, clarity and caret weight. To say that one criterion of a diamond is superior to another is shortsighted and irrational. Each criterion is important in its own right. The same is true with respect to religion. For example: Judaism, Christianity, Islam and other faith traditions should be compared to the best they have to offer to the world, and should not be compared to each other. When we compare two religions we risk falling into what the English philosopher John Stuart Mill (d. 1873) called "false analogy." False analogy arises when we compare apples and oranges. Yes, they are both fruits, they have outer skin, they come from trees, they have similar colors, but they cannot be practically compared. Have you ever heard of an apple that is faulted for not being a good orange?

To say that one faith is superior to another is akin to saying that a diamond's color is superior to a diamond's clarity (or akin to saying that apples are superior to oranges). As adherents of various faiths we should appreciate our own faith and have room in our hearts for what is equally beautiful and valid in other traditions. And just like diamonds are not compared based on different criteria, meaning a diamond's color is not compared to another diamond's cut, but only compared to its color, so too with religion. Christianity should be compared with what is best in Christianity. Islam should be compared with what is best in Islam and Judaism should be compared with what is best in Judaism. After all we have three different languages; and the Hebrew text can be compared, contrasted, improved upon and exegeted using only another Hebrew text. The same is true with Greek and Arabic texts. The Noble Koran teaches this concept in Chapter 5, verse 48.

As Qatada stated, *"al din wahid, we al sharia muchtalifa"* [7] – there is one *Deen*, and many (acceptable) *Shari'as*.[8] This means that Muslims can accept Jews and Christians, and Noachides as following the universal *Deen* that is binding on all humanity, and doing so via their respective covenants - their *Shari'a*. The Jews call *Deen* "The Noachide covenant", while their specific covenant is *Halacha* law. The Catholics refer to their covenant as Canonical law and the Muslims call theirs *Shari'a* law.

We can regard the conflict as a quarrel not between foreign elements, but as between the followers of the same religion but two different *Shar'ia*. Once Muslims and Jews view each other as members of the same *Deen*, just following different and acceptable *Shari'a*, dialogue will occur in the realm of the familiar. Both the Holy Qur'an and the Hadith declare that both are following different and acceptable Sharia.[9]

Sacred place, validating the other

One aspect of the conflict concerns what each faith claims as holy places in the Holy Land. There is resentment in the Jewish camp due to the refusal of the Arab and Muslim world to acknowledge the legitimacy of the Jewish state, regarding all of Palestine as an Islamic *Waqf* (endowment).[10] Such claims have led to a sense of a "right of possession" and the right to "envision" the Holy Land by both Jews and Muslims.

One way out of these conflicting views is to seek our commonalities. The Abrahamic faiths teach their adherents to emulate the character of the Prophet or Messenger that was assigned to them. Emulation, imitation, and drawing parallels are taken seriously when one identifies specific points of correspondence among the different religions. These points of correspondence become so much more alive when they involve scriptural people, events and places. Such places include, for example, where a prophet lived or where holy scripture was revealed. The tomb of the prophet Samuel is shared by both Muslims and Jews as a holy place, as is the Tomb of the Forefathers in Hebron.

A plan for lasting resolution would, therefore, require recognition and support of the "other" as a believer, perhaps not in what Muslims regard as the final revelation, but a divine revelation nonetheless. This includes validation of what the other camp holds as sacred space.

Emphasizing mutual goodwill, supported by their respective scriptures and beliefs, empowers all parties in the conflict, granting the tools to focus less on past injustices, differing perceptions of history, or rights of possession and sovereignty, and more on a hopeful future. A major step in this direction is what is basic to both Islam and Judaism – the Noachide covenant.

The Seven Noachide Laws

The Noachide Laws are seven categories of laws considered by rabbinic tradition as the minimal moral duties binding on all humanity.[11] The seven laws parallel the Ten Commandments – basic precepts on which religion is based.[12] Just like the 613 commandments that are binding upon Jews are based upon the Ten Commandments, hundreds of commandments are derived from the seven laws that are binding upon the nations of the world. Every non-Jew who accepts these obligations is considered a righteous person who is guaranteed a place in the world to come.[13]

These laws are:

> Do Not Deny God
>
> Do Not Blaspheme God
>
> Do Not Murder

Do Not Engage in Incestuous, Adulterous
or Homosexual Relationships.

Do Not Steal

Do Not Eat the limb of a Live Animal

Establish Courts of Justice

Except for the seventh law, all are negative commands, and the last itself is usually interpreted as commanding the enforcement of the others. They are derived exegetically from divine edicts addressed to Adam and Noah, the progenitors of all mankind, and are thus regarded as universal.[14]

Noachides may also freely choose to practice certain other Jewish commandments, and Maimonides (d. 1204)[15] held that Noachides must not only accept these seven laws on their own merit, but must also accept them as divinely revealed.[16]

The prohibition of idolatry provides that the non-Jew does not have to "know God" but must disregard false gods.[17] This law refers only to actual idolatrous acts but, unlike Jews, Noachides are not required to suffer martyrdom rather than break this law. They are, however, required to choose martyrdom over murder. The Tosefta records four possible additional prohibitions against: (1) drinking the blood of a living animal; (2) emasculation; (3) sorcery; and (4) all magical practices listed in the book of Deuteronomy 18:10-11.[18]

Even though the Talmud and Maimonides stipulate that a non-Jew who violated the Noachide laws was liable for capital punishment,[19] contemporary authorities have expressed the view that this is only the maximal punishment. According to this view, there is a difference between Noachide law and *halacha*.[20] According to *halacha*, when a Jew was liable for capital punishment it was a mandatory punishment, provided that all conditions had been met, whereas in Noachide law death is the maximal punishment, to be enforced only in exceptional cases.

In view of the strict monotheism of Islam, Muslims were considered as Noachides whereas the status of Christians was a matter of debate. Since the later Middle Ages, however, Christianity too has come to be regarded as Noachide, on the ground that Trinitarianism is not forbidden to non-Jews.

Commonalities Between Muslims and Jews

Both Muslims and Jews worship and revere the same God, the God of Abraham and Moses. Both Muslims and Jews affirm the absolute unity of God. Because the followers of the Prophet Muhammad are the majority in that area, in order to find a lasting peaceful solution to the conflict, one has to respond and alleviate the concerns of the Muslims and render them benign. There is no better way to do that than to exegete the Holy Qur'an in a way that allows for such peace to take place and support such exegesis with historical precedent.

The holy Qur'an teaches that all Ahlul Kitab – the people of the book - are Muslims (hence: it is possible to view God-fearing Jews as Muslims). The Qur'anic texts that denote such relationship can be found in the twenty eighth chapter of the Qur'an (Q28:52-53) as follows:

الَّذِينَ آتَيْنَاهُمُ الْكِتَابَ مِن قَبْلِهِ هُم بِهِ يُؤْمِنُونَ وَإِذَا يُتْلَى عَلَيْهِمْ قَالُوا آمَنَّا بِهِ إِنَّهُ الْحَقُّ مِن رَبِّنَا إِنَّا كُنَّا مِن قَبْلِهِ مُسْلِمِينَ.

"Those to whom We sent the Book before this (Ahlul Kitab),- they do believe in this (revelation): And when it is recited to them, they say: "We believe therein, for it is the Truth from our Lord: indeed we have been Muslims (bowing to Allah's Will) from before this."

In turn, the Talmud teaches that Muslims are ethical monotheists (Hence: it is possible to view God-fearing Muslims as Jews). The texts that denote such relationship can be found in the Talmud, Tractate Megilah 13 as follows:

כל מי שמכחיש אלילים נקרא יהודי

"Whosoever denies idols is called a Jew."

From searching the Hebrew Bible and the Holy Quran one could deduce that both Muslims and Jews believe the following:[21]

1. We believe that God is an absolute simple unity without parts or likeness of any kind.

2. We believe that God has communicated to humanity through prophets.
3. We believe that humanity relates to God, even to the extent that we know God's will for us through the medium of law, through divine commandments revealed in scripture, and understood through certain oral traditions and, to varying degrees, logical reasoning.
4. We believe that God cares as much about how we interact with other people as God cares about how we interact with God.
5. We believe in regular prayer at set times with set liturgy, a spiritual script recited multiple times daily.
6. We believe that God wants us to dedicate ourselves to Him in all areas of our life, even including eating, drinking, sleeping and marital relations.
7. We believe that man is the "viceroy" of God in this world, the pinnacle of creation who bears a special responsibility for this world.
8. We believe that our actions matter, and have implications that go beyond this life in the form of reward and punishment after death.
9. We believe that life is a purposeful journey tailor-made just for us, including its most difficult trials.
10. We believe that in matters of moral choice we are given free will by our Creator.
11. We believe that part of the mission of mankind is to create ever more perfect societies.
12. We believe that the property of other people is precious and that business should be done with the utmost of integrity.
13. We believe that our actions shape us and make us who we are.

14. We believe that giving to others in the form of both charity and acts of kindness are pillars of what it means to be truly human.
15. We believe that out of self-respect should emerge modesty and true humility.
16. We believe that the physical distinction between male and female is spiritually significant, giving rise to somewhat different practices for men and women and varying degrees of gender segregation when deemed appropriate.
17. We believe that religious action should be infused with intention.
18. We believe that the religion that God commands is moderate and balanced.
19. We believe that extremism, especially violent extremism, is an aberration and distortion of faith.
20. We believe that peace is our highest value and that without peace we are unable to enjoy the many gifts which God gives us.
21. We believe in supporting and defending the most vulnerable in society - the widows and orphans.
22. We believe in engaging in a profound spiritual struggle against our lower selves, unworthy motivations, and desires.
23. We believe that awe of God and love of God are both modes of service.
24. We believe that the highest calling of mankind is to be a servant or slave to God.
25. We believe that the greatest fruit of free will is to be obedient to God.
26. We believe that all greetings begin with peace and all prayers end with peace.
27. We believe that without peace, we are collecting G-d's blessings with a damaged vessel, a leaky bucket.

28. We believe in the sanctity of time and place.
29. We believe that the Messiah / Moshiach / Mahdi is destined to arrive and bring completion to humanity.

Uniqueness of Each Revelation

When it comes to the question of why there is a need for new revelations, two reasons are often cited: first, the new revelations were given because the old revelations became corrupted through distortion, misrepresentation, or falsification. Second, new revelations were given because of the natural diversity of humankind. Each nation must follow the same *Deen* (basic universal law), but was also given its specific Prophet, Book, and *Shari'a* (covenant). Allah could have created us a single nation *(ummah)* but He chose not to:

> "... to each among you have we prescribed a shari'a and minhaj (custom). If Allah had so willed, He could have made you a single ummah, but (Allah's plan is) to test you in what Allah hath given you: so strive as in a race in all virtues. The goal of you all is to Allah; it is Allah that will show you the truth about the matters in which ye differ."[22]

> "We sent not a Law Giver, a messenger, except to teach in the language of his own people, in order to make things clear to them: and Allah is Exalted in power, full of Wisdom."[23]

> "Had Allah sent this Qur'an in a language other than Arabic, they would have said: "Why are not its verses explained in detailed Arabic?"[24]

The Prophet Muhammad echoed the same message when he said:

> "From amongst all those nations (*ummahs*) you are among the *ummah* that has been allotted to me and from amongst all the prophets I am the prophet who hath been assigned to you."[25]

Religion and government

Professor Eric Nelson of Harvard University makes the point that the architects of the British and American governments patterned themselves after the deeply religious ancient Hebrew republic. In agreement with the views of Swiss theologian Thomas Erastus (d. 1583), they held that punishments should only be meted out by a civil magistrate, and not a religious body, and only when essential to the functioning of society. They envisioned a bicameral parliamentary system where the lower house would represent the needs and desires of the general population, while the upper house would represent the rights and obligations of the people to God. Together these houses would make laws.[26]

English jurist John Seldon (d. 1654) patterned the House of Lords after the ancient Jewish Sanhedrin. What this means is that only in relatively recently history has religious authority not been given a voice in government. Just as taxation without representation led to revolution, so to religious conscience without representation inevitably leads to expressions of religious fanaticism which is uncontrolled and outside the bounds of government. For example, the suppression of religious expression during the rule of Mubarak in Egypt gave rise to many extremist Islamic organizations such as Islamic Jihad and Al Qaeda headed by Ayman al Zawahiri.

As to the Arab-Israeli conflict, it is interesting that both sides are making claims on the land based on their understanding of their respective sacred text. A Palestinian may object here and say no, while the Israeli claim is based on a literal and selective reading of the Tanakh, the Palestinian claim is based on deeds to their lands and houses in addition to text in the Holy Qur'an. Professor Sallama Shaker at Yale Divinity School is renowned for saying, "if you are making a claim, show me the text."[27] Well there is plenty of sacred text on the Israeli side, and sacred and secular text on the Palestinian side, which show that God gave the land to the Children of Abraham. Both sides claim to be the rightful heirs of the promise to the Patriarch Abraham. However, both Hebrew and Arabic religious texts say that all the Earth belongs to God. God appoints certain people who are close to God as guardians of the land for a prescribed period of time.[28]

Religious leaders are marginalized from the political sphere, and politicians do not base their politics on religious text. That is why all political solutions to the conflict over the last seventy years have failed, and will continue to fail until a religious solution is found based on religious text.

Dignitism and Peace

What could happen if we believed that there is more than one way to worship God and be a good human being? One may call such belief "dignitism."

What could happen if we believed that the Prophet Moses received from Allah on Mt. Sinai a superior way for human beings to worship Allah and live their lives as recorded in the Hebrew Torah, and recognized that the Torah also says that in Allah's vast universe there are other people who worship Allah, and are equally acceptable to Him? [29]

What could happen if we believed that Jesus received from Allah on Mt. Carmel a superior way for human beings to live their lives and worship Allah as recorded in the Greek Gospel, and recognized that the Greek Gospel also says that in Allah's vast universe there are other people who worship Allah who are equally acceptable to Allah? [30]

What could happen if one considers that the Prophet Muhammad received from Allah on Mt. Hira'a a superior way for human beings to live their lives and worship Allah,[31] and recognized that the Arabic Qur'an also says that in Allah's vast universe there are other people who worship Allah who are equally acceptable to Allah? [32]

What could happen if one believes that people who sincerely follow Moses, Jesus, or Muhammad are equally acceptable by Allah?

What could happen if religious leaders set aside the idea of supersession (one religion negating all other religions)?

What could happen if religious leaders believe with certainty the fact that Allah said that He intentionally sent different prophets in different languages to different people to test all of us?[33] What could happen if one believed in dignitism?

What could happen if one thought that Christians believe in the unity of God just as Muslims and Jews believe in the unity of God, but in a slightly different way?

What could happen if one thought that pious Jews and Christians believe in angels just as Muslims believe in angels?

What could happen if one thought that pious Jews believe that the Hebrew Torah is the word of God just as Muslims believe that the Qur'an is the word of God?

What could happen if one thought that Christians believe that the Greek Gospel is the word of God just as Muslims believe that the Arabic Qur'an is the word of God?

What could happen if one thought that pious Jews love and revere their Prophet Moses just as Muslims love and revere the Prophet Muhammad? What could happen if one thought that Christians love and revere Jesus just as Muslims love and revere the Prophet Muhammad? Can religious leaders then have a place in their hearts for each other? Can religious leaders truly ponder and apply the verse in the Holy Qur'an that Allah sent different guides to different people?[34]

What could happen if Jews, Christians, and Muslims would in turn regard the various paths *within* their peoples as acceptable?

What could happen if Muslims believed that there is more than one way to Allah? Allah said in the Qur'an that there are many ways to Him. Therefore, one should be thankful to Allah for all his blessings, including the blessing of creating people of other faith traditions.

According to the Prophet Muhammad, a Muslim's paradise is beneath the feet of non-Muslims including Christians and Jews.[35] One's faith in Islam is not really tested until one has a Jewish neighbor on one side and a Christian neighbor on the other side, and one is kind and respectful to both of them. Some Christian and Jewish neighbors may actually be moved by such gestures; they may even start investigating Islam.

For those wary of assimilation, I quote the *hadith* Ahmad Nasai, "Heaven lies under the feet of the mother." Strong relationships in the home are key, keeping one's children on the path set out by their parents. Kindnesses to neighbors of other faiths will thus not threaten your integrity; quite the opposite—they will be most pleasing to the Creator.

Rabbi Adin Steinsaltz, known as the "once-in-a-millennium scholar,"[36] in his "The Irrelevance of Toleration" argues in favor of finding a common foundation and allowing for diversity.[37] He states this is a better solution than toleration, which implies withholding condemnation for doing something wrong.

That is dignitism.

Summary

In sum, the possible religious solutions to the conflict require embracing some key assumptions – and they are:

1. A recognition of the great reverence in which scripture is held by the peoples of the Middle East. Revitalize the awareness of the Biblical roots of modern western political theory as set down by Thomas Luber Erastus and his followers.
2. View all people of the region as Ahlul Kitab, people of the book, and part of an *Umma Wahida*[38] that shares a common *Deen* with various *Sharia*. In this vein, joint Muslim-Jewish courts will adjudicate disputes, interpreting the Islamic and Jewish traditions to create a unified legal system.
3. Utilize semantics that are comfortable to all parties involved, for example, favoring terms such as "Holy Land" and "Ahlul Kitab".
4. Recognition and support for the sacred spaces of Islam, Judaism, and Christianity, as well as for the personal examples set by the prophets for the respective groups.
5. A living understanding of Noachide law.
6. A living recognition of the many commonalities between Islam and Judaism.

7. Utilizing Dignitism and a path to peace.

But these solutions cannot be implemented in a vacuum. Various issues must be put into context. The Holy Qur'an says that the best policy is honesty.[39] President Obama echoed this Qur'anic sentiment when he outlined:

> "In order to move forward, we must say openly to each other the things we hold in our hearts and that too often are said only behind closed doors. There must be a sustained effort to listen to each other; to learn from each other; to respect one another; and to seek common ground . . . It's easier to blame others than to look inward. It's easier to see what is different about someone than to find the things we share. But we should choose the right path, not just the easy path. There's one rule that lies at the heart of every religion—do unto others as you would have them do unto you."[40]

President Obama is inviting all sides to what scholars term "eminent criticism" – honest dialogue which gets to the root of the problems.[41] Thus, one has to look at the plight of the Arab Palestinians and the plight of the Arab Jews, then, answer questions like: what is the purpose of the Holy Qur'an? What does the Qur'an say about the plight of both peoples? What is the concept of Holy Land in the Holy Qur'an? I will attempt to answer these questions. First, let us look at the relationship of the Jewish people to the Holy Land.[42]

---

1 - Peter L. Burger, *The Desecularization of the World*, (Michigan: Wm. B. Eerdmans Publishing, 1999) p. 2.
2 - Joseph Berger, "Aided by Orthodox, [NY} City's Jewish Population Is Growing Again", New York Time, June 12, 2012.
3 - Darrell G. Young, Focus on Jerusalem, Prophecy Ministry. www.focusonjerusalem.com.
4 - Muhammad, prophet of Islam. The Columbia Encyclopedia, Sixth Edition. 2001-07
5 - It is important to familiarize ourselves with the writings of Thomas Luber Erastus, John Selden, the founding fathers of the United States, and other political theorists of sixteenth through eighteenth century Europe. Modern western political science was based on these theorists' concepts of the ancient Hebrew commonwealth, a fact often overlooked in the west. إنَّ الدِّينَ عِندَ اللَّهِ الْإِسْلَامُ
6 - **The Religion before Allah is Islam** (submission to God's Will)" Qur'an 3:19.
7 - Qatada was a companion of Muhammed (pbuh)
8 - **"To each among you have we prescribed a covenant and an open way."** Qur'an 5:48

9 - Qur'an 3:113, 7:159, 5:48
10 - David Meir-Levi, Lecturer at San Jose University, via email dated June 13, 2012
11 - Source: Encyclopedia Judaica, Jewish Virtual Library: Religion.
12 - Though the terms "Bible" and "Old Testament" are commonly used by non-Jews to describe Judaism's scriptures, the appropriate term is "Tanach," which is derived as an acronym from the Hebrew letters of its three components: Torah, Nevi'im and Ketuvim.
13 - Noah was the son of Lamech and born ten generations after Adam. The Torah relates that "Noah was a righteous man in his generation" (Genesis 6:9) and thus spared the fate of all humanity at that time to the earth's destruction by water. Noah builds an ark at God's command, and takes his wife, sons Shem Ham and Japheth, and his son's daughters into the ark. The ark also saves a male and female of each animal. (Genesis 7) After 150 days of floating, the ark lands on Mount Ararat. When they enter on dry land, Noah and his family prepare sacrifices to God. God promises that he will never again destroy the earth through flood. He shows the family a sign of his eternal covenant: A rainbow. He dies at age 950.
14 - Adam was the first man, created by God. (Genesis 2:7). Man is described in the Torah as a likeness of God and also as a worker of the ground. From Adam's rib God formed his wife Eve (Genesis 2:21), and he placed the couple in the Garden of Eden. After eating from the forbidden fruit, both Adam and Eve were expelled (Genesis 3:17-24). As a punishment he was forced to work for a living and to die at the time God chooses. Adam and Eve had three children, two of whom were the famous pair of Cain and Abel and another son named Seth.
15 - Moshe ben Maimon (Hebrew: משה בן-מימון), or Mūsā ibn Maymūn (Arabic: موسى بن ميمون), acronymed Rambam; a preeminent medieval Sephardic Jewish philosopher and astronomer, became one of the most prolific and influential Torah scholars.
16 - Maimonides was the first person to write a systematic code of all Jewish law, the Mishneh Torah; he produced one of the great philosophic statements of Judaism, The Guide to the Perplexed; published a commentary on the entire Mishna; served as physician to the sultan of Egypt; wrote numerous books on medicine; and, in his "spare time," served as leader of Cairo's Jewish community.
17 - Greek: ειδωλολατρεία eidōlon originally meant "image" or "fantasy." By the time of the Septuagint the term was used for images of gods. "Idolatry" is literally "image worship." To grasp the character of image worship in biblical literature one must first realize that the Bible describes the worship of all "strange gods" as idolatry, or the worship of "wood and stone."
18 - TOSEFTA (Aram. תּוֹסֶפְתָּא, Heb. תּוֹסֶפֶת), literally an "additional" or "supplementary" halachic (legal) or aggadic (lore) tradition, i.e., one not included in the Mishnah of R.*Judah ha-Nasi. Originally the term was used to designate any individual additional or supplementary tannaitic tradition, and so was virtually synonymous with the later Babylonian term *baraita.
19 - Many of the crimes for which any biblical punishment is prescribed carry the death penalty. The three methods of executing criminals found in the Bible are stoning, burning, and hanging.
20 - The word "halachah" (from the root halach, "to go"), the legal side of Judaism (as distinct from aggadah, the name given to the non-legal material, particularly of the rabbinic literature), embraces personal, social, national, and international relationships, and all the other practices and observances of Judaism.
21 - The list is composed by Lee Weissman of Irvine, California and is endorsed by Professor Muhammad Al-Fiqui of Al Azhar University and by the author.
22 - Ibid Maida Q5:48

23 - Ibid Ibrahim Q14.4
24 - Ibid Fussilat Q41.44
25 - Hadith, Musnad Ahmed 2614
26 - The Hebrew Republic: Jewish Sources and the Transformation of European Political Thought (Harvard/Belknap, Hardcover 2010; Paper 2011).
27 - Sallama Shaker, "Religion, Globalization and the Arab Awakening of 2011," Yale Divinity School, class discussion, January 31, 2012.
28 - **Allah has promised, to those among you who believe and work righteous deeds, that Allah will, of a surety, grant them in the land, inheritance (of power), as Allah granted it to those before them"** Qur'an 24:55
29 - *The Harper Collins Study Bible*, Ecclesiastes 3:11 (New York: HarperCollins Publishers, 2006) p. 895.
30 - Ibid., Romans 1:20, p. 1912.
31 - Ghar Hira'a or Mount Hiraa is a place near present day Mecca, KSA.
32 - **"We did aforetime send apostles before thee: of them there are some whose story We have related to thee, and some whose story We have not related to thee."** Qur'an 40:78
33 - **"To each among you (Jews Christians and Muslims) we have prescribed a law and an open way. If Allah had so willed, Allah would have made you [Jews, Christians and Muslims] a single people, but Allah's plan is to test you in what Allah has given you: so strive as in a race for all virtues."** Qur'an5:48
34 - **"We sent you [O Mohammed] only as a harbinger, and to every people [such as Jews and Christians] we have sent a guide."** Qur'an13:7
35 - **"Wherewith Allah guides all who seek His good pleasure to ways of peace and safety, and leads them out of darkness, by His will, unto the light."** Ibid. Qur'an 5:16.
36 - "If a human being is guided to the path of Allah because of your efforts, you will be rewarded with paradise" *Sahih Muslim Book* (Cairo: Hadith Publications, 2009) Hadith number 2406 - paraphrased.
37 - Richard N. Ostling (18 January 1988). "Giving The Talmud to the Jews," Time Magazine. Retrieved 23 April 2010.
38 - *Umma Wahida* means "United Nation"
39 - **O ye who believe! Fear Allah and be with those who are honest and fruitful.** Q9:119.
40 - Barack Obama, *"Remarks by the President on a New Beginning"*, Cairo University, Cairo, Egypt, June 4, 2009, On Line.
41 - Longe O, Maratos FA, Gilbert P, Evans G, Volker F, Rockliff H, Rippon G. (2010). Having a word with yourself: Neural correlates of self-criticism and self-reassurance. Neuroimage. 49:1849 –1856.
42 - Please see Exhibits 4, 5 and 6 for possible land swaps in the Holy Land and historic map of the Twelve tribes of Israel.

Sheikhs & Rabbis
IN ZEFAT, ISRAEL

Mayor Ilan Shohat, Omer Salem, Sheikh Ahmed Adwan and Chief Rabbi Eliyahu

The Jews and the Land

Adapted from my presentation at the Israeli Parliament (Knesset)
July 2012

In the Jewish tradition, which holds the Torah as the Word of God, the Laws of Torah govern both personal and public life, forming a complete way of living that enabled the Jews to operate without sovereignty for most of their history. Thus, concepts of possession of the Land of Israel were suspended until a hoped-for future restoration.

This is why the Children of Israel have been able to operate as a stateless people in the diaspora for many more years than they operated as a sovereign state. As long as the requirements of the Torah were met, the Jews had "sufficient" sovereignty. However, this was never deemed as a full actualization of the Jewish religion, as there are many commandments that are observed only in the Holy Land, for example, regarding agriculture and the festivals.

Thus, an ingathering of the exiles to the Holy Land and sovereignty was always longed for by many Jews world-wide.

Concerning agriculture, every seven years the land must lie fallow, no cultivation of crops is permitted. This is referred to as the *"shemitta"* year, and is based upon the commandments in Leviticus 25:1-7, Leviticus 26:34, and Exodus 23:10-12. " . . . and the land shall rest a Sabbath to the Lord" (Leviticus 25:1). *Shemitta* is considered a test of faith for the farmer, who for an entire year must refrain from working the land. Produce that grows naturally is considered ownerless and can be gathered by anyone.

The observance of Jewish festivals differs in the Holy Land; there they are observed for one day, while outside the Holy Land, festivals are observed for two days. (The exception is *Rosh HaShana*, the New Year, which is observed for two days in the Holy Land as well.) The historical explanation has to do with the effectiveness of communicating the sighting of the new moon to communities outside the Land. When the new moon was sighted in the Holy Land by two witnesses, beacons on successive hills were lit to carry the message abroad. Rival groups sabotaged the beacons, rendering the message unreliable. The Rabbis then mandated that festivals be observed for two days outside the Holy Land to ensure that the message of the sighting of the new moon reached Jewish communities abroad accurately.

The subjective feelings of many Jews across the spectrum for the Holy Land cannot be overlooked. From the secular to the religious, you will hear members of the Jewish community relate their special feelings of attachment to the land, whether they dwell in it or not. A plane landing in Israel will be the scene of Jews clapping enthusiastically; many kiss the ground upon disembarking.

World wide anti-Semitism has been another impetus for the perceived need for the Jewish people to have a country. They needed to have a place free of oppression or subjugation by other peoples as delineated to them in the Three Oaths Midrash. The concept of "sufficient sovereignty" became insufficient sovereignty when Jews became increasingly oppressed and when politics intervened. In 1917, as the Ottoman Empire, which at the time ruled the Holy Land, was nearing its demise, Arthur Balfour, the Foreign Secretary of Great Britain issued the Balfour Declaration:

> "His Majesty's government view with favor the establishment in Palestine of a national home for the Jewish people, and will use their best endeavors to facilitate the achievement of this object, it being clearly understood that nothing shall be done which may prejudice the civil and religious rights of existing non-Jewish communities in Palestine, or the rights and political status enjoyed by Jews in any other country."[1]

In a rational world, this declaration would have been a win-win for both Jews and Arabs, because it envisions and promotes safety and security for the Jews while assuring civil and religious rights for the non-Jews. However, in 1939, at the onset of World War II, and for political reasons, Great Britain retracted on its promise:

> "A policy paper issued by the British government under Neville Chamberlain in which the idea of partitioning the Mandate for Palestine . . . was abandoned in favor of creating an independent Palestine governed by Palestinian Arabs and Jews in proportion to their numbers in the population"[2]

From the Balfour Declaration to the Chamberlain Declaration, one could clearly see the role of power politics in the granting of part of historical Palestine to the Jews, and then withdrawing such a grant.

According to Islam, the concept of sovereignty is non-territorial, transcendental, beyond human agency, indivisible, inalienable and truly absolute. God, the sovereign, is the primary lawgiver, while agents such as the Islamic state and the Caliphate enjoy marginal autonomy necessary to implement and enforce the laws of their sovereign.[3] Both the Holy Torah and the Holy Qur'an define possession and sovereignty in terms that have nothing to do with land ownership, land possession or land control.[4] Both say that land belongs to God—not to nations, principalities, kingdoms or states.[5]

In a secular world, where considerations on what the Bible or the Qur'an says are secondary, a concept such as land for peace is conceivable. However, in the Middle East, we no longer live in a secular world. That is why negotiations centered on land for peace are not effective. Such negotiations only serve to embolden extremists on both sides. For example: Zionist extremists say, "look how small the area of the State of Israel is, we did not occupy anyone's land, we were granted land by the United Nations. We should not give up land to anyone, and we will settle the land, from the river to the sea, by force if necessary".[6] A member of this camp may add that Israel has been willing to give up land, and has given up land, and has offered to give up more land; and every Israeli government from Ben Gurion to Netanyahu has pleaded for peaceful resolution and has resorted to force only after lethal provocation.[7]

To the above, a nationalist Arab may say "the Zionists have no regard for the inhabitants of Palestine. They colonized and occupied all of Palestine by force and renamed it Israel; and now they are negotiating to give us a small piece back so they can keep the rest of our land. We will not allow that to happen, we want all our land back—from the river to the sea—via peaceful negotiations or by force."

Both the Holy Torah and the Holy Qur'an delineate possession and sovereignty in terms that have nothing to do with commonly known concepts of land ownership.[8] Both say that land belongs not to nations, principalities, kingdoms or states, but to God alone.

Embracing Islam and Judaism's shared concepts of the transcendence of the Land will remove the focus from dividing up what really is not ours to divide. This will prevent the radicalization in both the Jewish and Arab communities. Energies will then be free to pursue peaceful coexistence as God would have it.

The Three Oaths

The Three Oaths is the popular name for a *Midrash*[9] found in the Talmud, which relates that God adjured three oaths upon the nations of the world. Two of the oaths pertain to the Jewish people, and one of the oaths pertains to the other nations of the world. The Jews for their part were sworn not to migrate from Exile to the Land of Israel *en masse* and not to rebel against the other nations, and the other nations in their turn were sworn not to subjugate the Jews excessively.

Amongst Orthodox Jews today there are primarily two different ways of viewing this *Midrash*. In the *Haredi* community, those who are strongly anti-Zionist often view this *Midrash* as not being fulfilled, whereas religious Zionists view it as having being fulfilled, and now obsolete. Both buttress their positions by citing historic rabbinic sources in favor of their view.

The context of the Talmudic dialogue containing the Three Oaths is a discussion in which attempts are made to defend Rav Zeira's desire to leave Babylon and go to the Land of Israel. It begins on tractate Ketubot 110b and continues on 111a (where the Three Oaths are plainly conveyed). The Gemarra quotes R. Yossi ben R. Chanina:

What are these Three Oaths?

One, that Israel should not storm the wall forcefully.

Two, the Holy One adjured Israel not to rebel against the nations of the world.

Three, the Holy One adjured the nations that they would not oppress Israel too much."[10]

This Midrash is an exegetical analysis of three separate verses in the Song of Songs, and naturally reflects the traditional interpretation, which sees the entire book as an allegory for the relationship between God and the Jewish people.

The above three oaths have formed the basis of Jewish anti-Zionist movements, such as Neturei Karta and the Satmar Hasidic group.

---

1 - Yapp, M.E. (1987-09-01). *The Making of the Modern Near East* 1792-1923. Harlow, England: Longman. p. 290.
2 - Manchester Guardian 24/5/39 pg.10.
3 - M.A. Moqtader Khan, "Sovereignty in Islam as Human Agency"
4 - Deuteronomy 10:14 **"Behold, to the LORD your God belong heaven and the heaven of heavens, the Land with all that is in it."**
5 - Qur'an 7:128 **for the Land is Allah's, to give as a heritage to such of His servants as He pleaseth; and the end is (best) for the righteous."**
5 - Qur'an 7:128 **for the Land is Allah's, to give as a heritage to such of His servants as He pleaseth; and the end is (best) for the righteous."**

6 - Baylis Thomas, The Dark Side of Zionism: Israel's Quest for Security Through Dominance (Maryland: Lexington Books, 2009) p45
7 - David Meir-Levi, Lecturer at San Jose University, via email dated June 13, 2012. Vol 1, No:10 (Dec 30, 1999)
8 - Qur'an 7: 128
9 - In Judaism, the *Midrash* (Hebrew: מדרש; plural *midrashim*) is the body of exegesis of Torah texts along with homiletic stories as taught by Chazal (Rabbinical Jewish sages of the post-Temple era) that provide an intrinsic analysis to passages in the Tanakh.
10 - ibid

THE OPPRESSED
OF THE LAND

Palestinian Refugees

From a lecture to graduates at the College of Languages and Translation, Al Azhar University, Cairo, Egypt January 2012

One question to be addressed is: what could happen if Arab governments set aside oppression of their own brethren? For example, what could happen if Arab leaders were to issue a formal apology to their Arab brothers and sisters who were forced to leave the Holy Land in 1948 and 1967 after the creation of the state of Israel? What could happen if Arab governments granted those displaced Holy Land Arabs unconditional full citizenship in all the Arab countries where they reside after having been displaced from their homes and their communities?

According to a 1999 survey of the Palestinian refugees, only about ten percent of Holy Land Arabs want to return to historical Palestine.[1]

However, until they are able to do so they should be offered citizenship in their country of birth or current residence. What could happen if Arab governments declared, "Sorry, we were wrong in excluding you, your children, and your grandchildren from employment in government, the military, civil service and seventy other professions," as is the case in at least a dozen Arab countries? [2] What could happen if Arab governments felt guilty for the orchestrated oppression they have been inflicting on those Holy Land Arabs? Why should Arab governments continue to keep those oppressed Arabs living in deplorable conditions in camps inside the Holy Land such as: Askar, Balata, Jenin, Tulkarm? [3] And in twenty-eight camps outside the Holy Land such as Marka, Shatila and Yarmuk? [4] Arab governments control almost a third of the world's wealth in the form of oil and gas production and reserves. Why can't Arab governments make life easier for them?

Likewise, what could happen if the state of Israel could set aside the oppression of its own inhabitants? What could happen if Israel issued a formal apology and granted those displaced Holy Land Arabs equal treatment where they reside after having been displaced from their homes and their communities? There are nineteen refugee camps in the West Bank, with over 740,000 residents, with overcrowding to such an extent that kids are growing up with no green space, and many schools operate in double shifts. Plus there are eight camps in the Gaza strip with over a million refugees. What could happen if Israel told the oppressed, "Sorry, we were wrong in mistreating you, your children, and your grandchildren as is the case around all 120 settlements in the West Bank? [5] What could happen if Jews worldwide felt ashamed of the oppression of those Holy Land Arabs? [6] What could happen if Jewish settlers in the West Bank uphold the verses in the Tanakh that prohibit mistreating one's neighbor? [7] Why should Israel continue to keep those oppressed Arabs living in deplorable conditions in camps inside the Holy Land? Political parties sympathetic with settlers hold almost a third of the Israeli Knesset seats, why can't they make life easier for the Holy Land Arabs?

It is rather pathetic that both Jewish and Muslim traditions call for treating the weak and the destitute with magnanimity, love and care; yet both the Israeli and Arab governments are doing exactly the opposite with the Holy Land refugees. The number of those refugees has grown from 915,000 people in 1950 to more than five million people in 2010.[8]

There are two reasons why the Israeli government will not allow those refugees to return en mass to their homes, for which many of them still have keys. The first reason is that many of those homes are now occupied by Arab Jews who were forced to leave the MENA region in the 1940s, 50s and 60s, whereupon an exchange of population occurred. Israel absorbed its Arab Jews – Arab states did not absorb the Palestinian refugees. The second reason is that there is general fear in Israel that returning refugees may form a fifth column, posing a demographic threat and sowing the seeds of the destruction of the Jewish state. (This fear will be completely jettisoned if Muslims and Jews can regard themselves as sharing the same *Deen*, just practicing different *Sharia*).

In another mockery of justice, the Palestinian Authority, which is funded mainly by US and EU,[9] considers a Palestinian who sells his land to a Jew as having committed treason and therefore guilty of a capital offense and deserving the death penalty.[10] Despite such laws,[11] when some Holy Land Arabs complain about social injustice in the Arab countries, then Arabs add insult to injury by accusing them of deserving their unbearable conditions in the refugee camps, because they allegedly sold their land to the Jews in Palestine.[12]

Leaving Holy Land Arabs to languish in refugee camps is not without its costs. The physical, emotional and mental suffering sustained by them exerts psychological pressure on other Arabs worldwide, from Rabat to Riyadh.[13] Remember, ninety-two percent of Arabs are Muslims. Thus, the pressure on the Arab world is organically influencing one billion Muslims worldwide, from Tangier to Timor. Many of those Muslims are led to hate Zionism, Jews and Israel even though the overwhelming majority of those hating Israel don't even know where Israel exists on a map. I was witness to such hatred among Indian Muslims as faraway as Kayalpatnam Mosque, in the State of Tamil Nadu region of India.[14]

Such pressure on Muslims is reflected in the near silence and even tolerance for "Suicide Martyrs" or what is commonly known in the west as "Suicide Bombers" or "Muslim Terrorists". This may be an over simplification, but it appears to me that while one group teaches intolerance towards Jews, Zionists and Israel, the other group retaliates by teaching intolerance towards Palestinians, Arabs and Muslims.

Radical Islam and the Conflict

Radical extremism throughout the Arab and Islamic worlds would be greatly reduced by solving the conflict in the Holy Land.[15]

In the West, radical Islam is perceived as synonymous with terrorism. The dictionary definition of terrorism is: *the use of violence and intimidation in the pursuit of political aims.* And each side points the finger at the other in terms of who fits that definition.

When some Arabs use violence to pursue what they claim as the political aim of social justice and self determination, Israel calls that terrorism, declaring that Palestinians do not want social justice, they want the destruction of the State of Israel. They point out that if Palestinians really wanted self determination, they could have had it on thirty-one different occasions since 1937.[16]

When some members of the Jewish population build illegal settlements in the West Bank, claiming both historical and security considerations, some members of the Arab population declare this to be violence and intimidation; the Arab media calls it State Sponsored Terrorism.[17] Arab and Muslim media likewise call the drone attacks employed by the United States government on Pakistani and Afghani targets as "state sponsored terrorism."[18] Both sides, the Arabs and the Israelis, are calling each other "terrorists", and both mean it sincerely.

Terrorism is costing the United States dearly. This includes long security lines at airports, metal detectors in all government buildings, and a general fear of traveling. Even United States embassies appear more and more like castles and garrisons with plenty of security details, guards, and even marines on staff.

This general feeling of fear in the West could all become part of history as Ahlul Kitab religious leaders collaborate to solve this nagging conflict.

The Palestinian Refugees

It is disheartening to realize that while Muslims claim to be followers of the Prophet Muhammad and his superb Islamic tradition, some tend to mistreat the weak among them, and use the feeblest of excuses to do so. The Holy Qur'an advises against such practice.[19] What is not acceptable to do with one's own sisters and brothers should also be an unacceptable when directed at the Holy Land Arabs.[20] Abandoning them to subhuman living conditions in refugee camps should be seen both as an embarrassment and as an opportunity to practice the Islamic concepts of charity (*zakat*), mercy, and benevolence in alleviating their plight.

Someone may say, but if Arab governments treat the Holy Land Arabs as equal citizens in Arab countries, this would dilute the concept of "right of return" for Palestinian refugees, and they would forget about returning to their homes. This excuse exacerbates the conflict.

Additionally, Arab governments are using the plight of the refugees in order to present the State of Israel as an existential threat.[21] They do this by portraying Israel as intent on expanding its borders and controlling all of the Middle East.[22] According to their logic, if Arab governments would give Palestinians their citizenship, Israel would expand and occupy the area between the Nile and the Euphrates, which includes parts of Egypt, parts of KSA, Jordan, Syria, Lebanon and Iraq.[23]

Regarding the concept of "occupation", there is support among some Arabs[24] and Jews[25] that it is the United States, not the Jews, who are in fact the occupiers. Activist Yehuda HaKohen, an orthodox Jew who resides in the west bank, declares that a Palestinian state would likely be an American-backed police state and would not serve the interests of anyone there.[26]

The Holiness of the Land from a Jewish perspective

The holiness of the land to the Jews refers to the observance of agricultural and festival laws. It is independent and unrelated to statehood. With or without a sovereign Jewish state, agricultural and festival laws were observed by Jews throughout the millennia in the

Holy Land. This independence of holiness and political sovereignty means that there is absolutely no requirement in Judaism to conquer any land that is considered holy but not right now controlled by the state of Israel.

Mainstream rabbis, both of the Haredi and Zionist camp, assert that the boundaries of the Holy Land are:

> East – Jordan River
>
> West – Mediterranean Sea
>
> North – below Damascus
>
> South – Beersheba

The land allotted to the twelve tribes by God in the Torah occupied a larger area, but the failure of the children of Israel to conquer all this territory meant that the boundaries of the land contracted to the above mentioned borders. All or part of the Holy Land may be under discussion, but nothing more.

The Jewish camp thus sees the claim that Israel wishes to conquer all the Middle East as patently absurd. According to Professor David Meir-Levi, no reputable Zionist has published a claim to any Arab land outside the boundaries of the Holy Land. However, Arab fears in this regard are based upon the following: (1) "Every place where you set your foot will be yours: Your territory will extend from the desert to Lebanon, and from the Euphrates River to the Mediterranean Sea." Deuteronomy 11:24; (2) the designs of the Israel flag (3) the shekel coin; (4) an exhibit in the Israeli Knesset which quotes Genesis 15:18, (5) and claims of odd Jews here and there considered to be a fringe element.[27] Thus, Jewish leaders may need to offer reassurance to the Arab world that their ambitions do not include territorial expansion, no matter how absurd that reassurance sounds to their own ears.

The claim made by Arab governments that Israel will expand and conquer all the Middle East is harped upon to sow fear in the hearts of their own people.[28] In fact, it is Israel and Zionism that is being constantly attacked by Arab and Muslim political leaders. For example, many Israelis claim that Ahmadinejad, former president of Iran, aims for the destruction of Israel. Indeed, Hamas claims "resistance till victory or martyrdom". Hezbollah's Musawi calls for "fighting [the Jews] not because we want something from you (Israel). We are fighting you because we want to destroy you", and Hassan Nasr 'Allah of Lebanon said to the Beirut Star newspaper: "we want all the Jews to come to Israel so that we don't need to go after them world-wide".[29] These political leaders clearly do not want peace. They only want Israel's destruction and the annihilation of the Zionist project. To those antagonists, no price is too high, not their people's lives, their own countries' economies, no price is too high to pay for the end goal of Israel's destruction.

The above is but a small taste of the cacophony emanating from both sides. The general feelings of fear in the west and in Israel, and of misery on the part of the Holy Land Arabs who dwell in refugee camps, spawn much of this animosity.

But there is a way out. The above issues could be history if religious and political leaders would collaborate to resolve this nagging conflict. Resolution should be done in the spirit of recognizing that we are all Ahlul Kitab/ people of the Book. We have to begin with religious leaders; agreement among religious leaders can then be brought to political leaders.

I will focus the next chapter on the indigenous people of historical Palestine, their plight, and ways out of that plight. Our next step: who are the Palestinian people and who is their legitimate representative?

---

1 - Khalil Shikaki, Results of Palestinian Survey Research (PSR) *Refugees' polls in the West Bank / Gaza Strip, Jordan and Lebanon on refugees' preferences and behavior in a Palestinian-Israelis Permanent Refugee Agreement,* Survey Research
2 - Unit: PSR Polls among Palestinian Refugees, 18 July 2003.
3 - Franklin Lamb, "The Case for Palestinian Right in Lebanon," Counterpunch website, April 20, 2011. 3 - UNRWA: Relief & Social Services Program, Amman Jordan and By William Wheeler, "Palestinians' bittersweet homecoming in Lebanon, *Christian Science Monitor,* 3/5/08. http:// csmonitor.com/World/Middle-East/2008/0305/p04s01-wome.html
4 - William Wheeler and Don Duncan, *World Politics Review,* March 11, 2008
5 - Ori Nir, Bankrolling Colonialism, (Jerusalem, Jordan Valley Press, 2010)
6 - Donald Macintyre, "No Changes on Racist Torah's King's Text", The Independent, Jerusalem, May 5, 2012
7 - Exodus 20:17 "You shall not covet your neighbor's Land." 8 - "And they feed, for the love of Allah, the indigent, the orphan, and the captive" Q76:8

8 - UNRWA: Relief & Social Services Program, Amman Jordan.
9 - US and EU fund about half of the PA budget. Fact Sheet: The Palestinian National Authority's Sources of Funding By MIFTAH, February 2006.
10 - Weiner, Justus Reid (2005). Human Rights of Christians in Palestinian Society. Jerusalem Center for Public Affairs. p. 22 and "PA court: Sale of Palestinian land to Israelis is punishable by death", Haarez, Sepember 12, 2010.
11 - Richard S. Levy, (2005). *Anti-Semitism: A historical encyclopedia of prejudice and persecution*. 2. ABC-CLIO. p. 31.
12 - Khaled Abu Toamah, "Contentions, the Palestinians Alone", Commentary, July 12, 2007
13 - Umm Kalthoum Abdu, "Nakba 2011: A Possible Trend-setter for the Upcoming Nakba
14 - In a small mosque called Zawya Shazlia in Kayalpatnam, the name of the 17th chapter of the Holy Qur'an was crossed with a pen and changed from B'nai Israel to Isra. When I asked Abdullah Qasemi, the Imam of the Masjid, why the name B'nai Israel was crossed, his answer was "Israel is a bad name".
15 - Alan Berger, Harvey Cox, Herbert C. Kelman ,Lenore G. Martin, Everett Mendelsohn, Augustus Richard Norton, Henry Steiner, Stephen M. Walt Israel and Palestine: Two States for Two people, if not now when? Boston Study Group on Middle East Peace.
16 - David Meir Levi, "31 Opportunities for Statehood Squandered in Favor of Genocide", Front Page Magazine, July 15, 2011
17 - Erdoğan accuses Israel of state terrorism, Today's Zaman, June 1, 2010
18 - Craig Mackenzie, U.S. drone strike kills 10 suspected militants in Pakistan as they 'console' family of commander killed in attack the day before, Prison Planet, June 3, 2012
19 - **The Believers are but a single Brotherhood:**" Q49:10 All Qur'anic verses in this book are done using Abdullah Yûsuf Ali, *The Meaning of the Holy Qur'an* (Maryland: Amana Publications, 2009)
20 - The Prophet of Islam said: **"the likening of the believers in their mutual love, sympathy and mercy is like the body, if a small part is hurting, the whole body reels in fever until that part is healed."** Imam Nawawi, Ryadul Saleheen (Cairo: Al Darul Hadith 2010) 65.
21 - Genesis 15:18 - **"To thy seed I have given this land, from the river of Egypt to the Great River, the river Perat . . . "** Deutoeronmy 11:24 – **"Every place whereon the sole of your foot shall tread shall be yours, from the wilderness to the Levanon, from the river, the river Perat, to the uttermost sea shall be your border."** John Tirman, The "Existential Threat" to Israel Is Israel", Huff Post World, March 3, 2012.
22 - Michael B. Oren , Seven Existential Threats, Commentary, May 2009.
23 - Daniel Pipes , Imperial Israel: The Nile-to-Euphrates Calumny, Middle East Quarterly, March 1994
24 - Arutz Shafer, "PA portrays US as Occupier," By Tova Dvorin, August 28, 2015.
25 - "Former Israeli Soldier Eran Efrati Speaks Out About Documenting IDF Abuse in Gaza, West Bank." Democracy Now, September 12, 2014.
26 - Yehuda adds that Israel should stop taking American money and American weapons and promote better relations with its neighbors https://www.youtube.com/watch?v=zc8fYgC86rA
27 - This website was made by a single Jew, and is not supported by any mainstream Jewish group: http://www.globalsecurity.org/ military /world/ Israel/ greater-israel-maps.htm
28 - David Meir-Levi, lecturer on the history of Zionism, San Jose University, via e-mail dated June 13, 2012.
29 - "The Enemy Within", *New York Times*, May 23, 2004.

Replace PLO
with HLCO

The Palestinian people are the people who inhabited the area between the Mediterranean coast and the Jordan River, commonly known as Palestine. Palestinians are represented in the international community by the Palestine Liberation Organization (PLO), founded in 1964 by the Arab League — a regional organization which now includes 22 Arab states and the PLO.[1]

The PLO has a name, a mission and a purpose, and from a political point of view its name mission and purpose may be beneficial, but, from a religious point of view, all three are harmful, more so to the PLO than to the State of Israel.

The PLO name is harmful because the land on which the PLO aspires to form a State is referred to in both the Holy Torah and the Holy Qur'an as "Holy Land"—not Palestine, and the term "Liberation" connotes war, in this case, against People of the Book. The mission is harmful because its goal is to establish a state for the people it represents—and control the flow of Jews running away from persecution and prevent them from reaching the Holy Land. The purpose is harmful because the PLO seeks to liberate the Holy Land from the very people who should be in the Holy Land when they have nowhere else to go, and who regard the Holy Land as the best place to keep God's commandments.

That is why the PLO has not been successful, from a religious point of view, in winning equality and social justice for the Palestinian people inside or outside the Holy Land. One may argue that the PLO's goals for social justice or equality were secondary to a more pressing priority: the struggle until victory (destruction of Israel) or martyrdom.[2]

If all three aspects of the PLO are harmful, what three aspects may the PLO consider to become benign? The Palestinian Liberation Organization (PLO) may consider changing its name to Holy Land Custodians Organization (HLCO). HLCO is much more beneficial than PLO. Why? The name Holy Land is more consistent with the Holy Scriptures than the term "Palestine". The concept of "custodian" denotes watching over, and it can imply serving and protecting the weak. Contrast that with the concept of "Liberating" which may imply war, incarceration and bondage. If Holy Land Arabs focus on guarding, helping and serving others, especially those running away from persecution, we all win.

The compelling reason to effect the name change for the PLO would be to stay true to the teachings of the Prophet Muhammad and the Holy Qur'an. God will be pleased that the PLO chooses a name, a mission and a purpose that brings it closer to the word of Allah as delineated in the Holy Qur'an. To convince the PLO leadership of the name change one would ask: Do you love Allah? Do you love the Prophet Muhammad? Do you want to draw yourself closer to Allah and His prophet? Yes. Change your name from PLO to HLCO and you will be drawing yourself closer to Allah and His prophet.

Therefore, going back to the Holy Land Arabs "right of return" – this must be balanced with the Arab governments' willingness to allow the scattered Arabs or Sephardic and Mizrahi Jews, who left—voluntarily or involuntarily—to return to their communities. That is, the Palestinian Arabs' right of return has to be balanced against the Arab Jews' right of return, which leads us to consider the plight of the Arab Jews who came to the Holy Land after being kicked out of their countries.

---

1 - Who represents the Palestinians officially before the world community? Institute for Middle East Understanding (IMEU).

2 - David Meir-Levi, Lecturer at San Jose University, via email dated June 13, 2012.

THE SCATTERED

IN THE LAND

Jewish Refugees

Adapted from my speech at the Tikkun conference
Jerusalem, December 2012

Professor Meir Buzaglo, head of the philosophy department
of Hebrew University, Jerusalem, invited me to speak at the
Tikkun conference after hearing my presentation
at the Israeli Knesset.

"A million Jews live in Egypt [and other Arab countries] and enjoy all the rights of citizenship, they have no desire to emigrate to Palestine. However, if a Jewish State were established, nobody could prevent disorder. Riots would break out in Palestine and spread through all the Arab States and may lead to a war between two races." [1]

These were the prophetic comments by Heykal Pasha, member of the Egyptian Delegate to the United Nations in April, 1947. As he predicted, a war broke out the following year. Close to half a million Holy Land Arabs were forced to leave, were evacuated, or ran for safety. As usual, there are two sides to this story. On the Arab side it is reported that the newly established Zionist State in Palestine caused the persecution and evacuation of those Holy Land Arabs. On the Israeli side, it is reported that those Holy Land Arabs picked up what they could carry with them and left their homes voluntarily to make room for Jews to come and live in Palestine. Arabs leaving voluntarily were considered by Israel to be stating that they did not wish to be ruled by Israel and to have relinquished their right of return. Arabs who stayed received Israeli citizenship.

In Arab circles this event is commemorated annually, on May 15th, as the Palestinian *Nakba* (catastrophe) Day. As a result of the *Nakba*, Jews in Arab Lands were affected in a negative way. A retaliatory policy was put in place in the Arab League to drive Arab Jews out of Arab Lands.[2] Following orders issued by the Arab League, outrageous acts were committed against Arab Jews from North Africa, Egypt, the Levant, Iraq, Iran, and Yemen.[3] For example, the Jews of Yemen complained that Jewish orphans were forced to convert to Islam. This contributed to the exodus from Yemen.[4] This is akin to the Christianization of Jewish orphans that took place in Spain in 1492.[5]

In the KSA, the Jews of Najran were offered (or forced) to leave the Kingdom on a specific day. On that specific day, KSA soldiers asked the Jews to hand their money over in order to protect it during the journey over land to the border. When the Jews arrived at the border, they asked for their money back. At that point they were told "the money had been confiscated by the Kingdom of Saudi Arabia," for under the Saudi Law it was forbidden to strengthen the State of Israel by money from KSA.[6]

In Iraq, law No. 1 of 1950 deprived Jews of their Iraqi nationality, and law No. 5 of 1951 deprived Iraqi Jews of their property. In Libya, by the time Colonel Gaddafi came to power, most Libyan Jews had fled the country. However, Gaddafi's immediate mission was to cleanse the nation of the few remaining Jews. In Syria, Jewish property was taken and appropriated and given to Arab refugees from the Holy Land. Holy Land Arabs were placed in houses in the Jewish ghetto in Damascus. In Egypt even highly respected members of the Jewish community were incarcerated and later expelled from Egypt. In Algeria, a mother of two Jewish boys came back home from shopping to find her two young boys in a pool of blood, their throats cut. This was the final provocation that made the Jews leave Algeria.[7]

Mr. Sabri Jiryis, director of the Institute of Palestine Studies in Beirut, summarized the condition of Arab Jews in an article published in the Beirut Daily AL-Nahar on May 15, 1975:

> "The State of Israel will raise the question in all serious negotiations that may in time be conducted over the rights of the Palestinians . . . Israel argument will take approximately the following form: it is true that we Israelis brought about the exodus of the Arabs from their land in Palestine in the war of 1948 . . . and that we took control of their property [and appropriated it to the Jews]. In return, however, you Arabs caused the expulsion of a like number of Jews from Arab countries since 1948. Most of them went to Israel after you seized control of their property one way or another. What happened is merely a kind of 'population and property transfer', the consequence of which both sides have to bear."[8]

Given the above unpleasant history of the Arab governments' treatment of their own citizens, the Arab Jews, What could happen if Arab governments considered the waves of Jewish people who came to the Holy Land in the 1940s and 1950s as people running away from danger, as people tired of oppression and subjugation, as people looking for self—determination - a place in the sun? What could happen if Arab governments thought that the Jews were persecuted in Europe and had nowhere else to go? What would happen if Arab governments finally acknowledge and believed that the Holocaust actually happened—and that in it one-third of all Jews were murdered?[9] What could happen if Arabs and Jews put into practice the ethical and moral values contained in their respective sacred text and forgave each other?[10]

While the Sephardic Jews came to the Holy Land because they were forced out by Arab governments in retaliation for the exodus of the Holy Land Arabs, the Ashkenazi Jews came to the Holy Land because they were persecuted and killed by the Nazi war machine in Europe in a horrific process called the Holocaust. Entire Jewish communities were annihilated in Germany, Poland, Russia, and other European countries.

The Jews are not unified as to how to explain the Holocaust. To the Orthodox, the Holocaust is a message from God to shun secular life. To the Zionists, the Holocaust is a message from God that Palestine must be made a Jewish home land - by force if necessary. To the secular, the Holocaust is a message that God is not in control or God does not exist.[11]

In the summer of 2011, on a trip to Kiev, Ukraine, I was a witness to one of the World War II horror stories; I visited to Babi Yar, where on Yom Kippur in 1941, the Nazis murdered more than 33,000 Jewish men, women, and children.[12] This showed that more Jews were killed in one day in Europe than all Jews killed in the seventy year conflict between Arabs and Jews. I fought back my tears as others in the group, some of whom had roots in the Jewish community of the Ukraine, sobbed openly as they mourned the loss of their families and very civilization.

No wonder the Jews wanted to leave Europe and come to settle among their Ishmaelite cousins in the Holy Land.

The Jews came to the Holy Land running away from danger. They came to take shelter among their cousins, the Arab descendants of Ismail. Allah put in the heart of the Jews that there was no safer place for the Jews to go except the Holy Land. Furthermore, Allah put in the hearts of some Christians (once the arch enemies of the Jews) the desire, perhaps out of guilt and remorse for the Holocaust, to support the Jewish people in their endeavor for safety and security. Muslims must come to grips with this phase of history and how it affected the Jewish nation.

Jewish refugees in history: finding safe haven in Muslim lands

The story of the Jews being outnumbered by their antagonists and running away from persecution has many precedents in history. The story of the Jewish Exodus was staged in Egypt, followed by the Babylonian exile, the Greek occupation, the Roman destruction, the European Crusades, the English expulsion, the Spanish Inquisition, the Russian pogroms and culminating with the German Holocaust.

THE SCATTERED IN THE LAND

Let us look at the Spanish Inquisition, when the Jews were expelled from Spain. Where did the Jews go? Where did the Jews run for cover? Where did they hide from danger? In Arab and Muslim lands. In 1492, when the Jews of Spain were told "convert or die" by King Ferdinand and Queen Isabella, they fled to Holland, North Africa, the Levant, Persia, modern day Iraq, and Anatolia. In 1492, Arabs and Muslims faced the same dilemma they are facing today. Namely, what to do with the Jews?[13] But did the Arabs oppose the Jews back then? Did they incite hatred against the Jews? Did they slaughter the Jews or pledge to feed the Jews to the fish in the sea? No! Arabs and Muslims sheltered the Jews, comforted the Jews, and made the Jews members of their society. My ancestors, who read and contemplated the word of Allah, found ample theological reasons to provide shelter for the Jews. Arabs and Muslims healed the wounds suffered by the Jews at the hands of the Spaniards.

One might ask, if that is true about the Muslims of the Ottoman Empire, how come many of the contemporary Muslims hate Israel? Contemporary Muslims hate Israel not because it offers a shelter for Jews running away from danger and not because it is a socialist and democratic nation. Contemporary Muslims hate Israel because they view Israel as a colonial power that descended on the Palestinian people, not to share the Holy Land, but to cleanse the Holy Land from all non-Jews, by force if necessary. According to Benjamin Abrahamson, "the fundamental difference between the Ottoman acceptance of Jewish refugees and the Zionist attempt to found a state was that under the Ottoman's the Jews were viewed as coreligionists, not as foreigners."[14]

Now let's think about this: Were those Arabs and Muslims who helped the Jews in 1492 mentally sluggish? Did they lack intelligence or good judgment when they provided shelter for the fleeing Jews? Were they not aware of the Holy Qur'an and Hadith traditions of the Prophet Muhammad? In fact, those Arabs were quite aware of the Qur'an and Hadith. They were actually wiser than the Arabs of the 1940s and 1950s, and they exercised good judgment. In fact, they used the Qur'an and Hadith as a basis to host and show integrity, kindness, and magnanimity to the Jews who were running away from danger on the Iberian Peninsula. The

Arabs were relying on Allah's commandments in the Holy Qur'an to provide the most precious commodity for those running away from persecution and danger - security.[15] "Security" is what the Spanish Jews were looking for five centuries ago when they fled to Arab land, and security is what the Jews are looking for today. As I said at the Tikkun conference, I am confident that, with the rise of Islamic leaning governments in the Middle East, adamant Muslims will be able to invoke Qur'anic text to effect security for the Jewish people.

History is repeating itself. This time the Jews are seeking security in our shared Holy Land. The majority of the Jews who came to the Holy Land are willing to share it with the Holy Land Arabs; only a small minority wants the whole land exclusively for the Jews. Likewise, the majority of the Holy Land Arabs are willing to share the Holy Land with the Jews; only a small minority wants the whole land exclusively for the Arabs.

Jewish security, Arab dignity

I have explained why in contemporary Western mainstream media, the adjective most associated with the Jews is "security," as in "the security of Jews" or "the security of Israel." Even when the Israeli army, the fourth largest army in the world, was bombarding Gaza in 2009, it was under the banner of "security needs", which was also used to explain why twelve hundred Arabs, mostly women and children were killed. Who is to blame? The State of Israel and its desire for security, or the Arab governments and their desire for dominance? What is amazing about this nearly seventy year old conflict between Arabs and Jews is that both sides of the conflict are talking about totally different causes. The Palestinians who live in the Holy Land are struggling for dignity and social justice, and the Jews who came to the Holy Land are struggling for safety and security. Arabs and Jews have two entirely different objectives. The Arabs are suing for dignity whereas the Jews are suing for security. Is that dichotomy clear? The conflict may include land, but the conflict is not entirely about the control of land. The conflict can thus be summarized as **Jewish security vs. Arab dignity.**

Some would say the conflict is also about geopolitical interests for the USA and EU members; however, the more Muslims and Jews work together, the more such interests can be deflected from the conflict. If Arab governments truly want dignity for the Holy Land Arabs, then they should find a way to restore security for the Jews. If one understands that, one could find a way to grant the Holy Land Jews their security while granting the Holy Land Arabs their dignity.[16] Moreover, despite the fact that some Arab Palestinians make fiery speeches about their desire to destroy the Zionist state, they are really fighting to live in dignity next to Israel.[17] This leads to a very important point about the Jews in Arab lands.

Jews in Arab Lands

> "Arabs didn't call themselves Palestinians until the Zionist movement began and Jews did not call themselves Israelis until the establishment of the state of Israel."[18]

There are many perspectives on how the State of Israel came to existence in Palestine. The State of Israel emerged from interaction with "the reality of war in Europe and the Jews' collective memory of being a scattered people seeking a homeland."[19] While the Zionists see the Holocaust as an organizing rationale for the State of Israel, [20] the international community views the 1947 partition plan as the basis for the creation of the State of Israel.

Let's consider the population of the state of Israel since its inception in 1948: its Jewish community consisted of Ashkenazi Jews and Sephardic Jews, about fifty percent each. Now, where did the Sephardic (Mizrahi, "eastern") Jews who reside now in the Holy Land come from? They came from Arab lands. They are Arab Jews who came from North Africa, the Levant, Iraq, Persia, and Yemen. Some Jews left Arab lands voluntarily to go to the Holy Land. However, the overwhelming majority of Jews in Arab lands loved their countries and did not want to leave,[21] they had lived there for many generations (in some cases more than 2500 years), and their parents, grandparents, and great grandparents are all buried there. The overwhelming majority of Jews in Arab lands were actually driven out against their will! The reasons for the involuntary exit of Jews from Arab lands included push factors such as persecution, anti-Semitism and political instability, together with pull factors, such as the desire to fulfill Zionist yearnings or find a better economic and secure future in Europe or the Americas. A significant proportion of Jews left due to political insecurity and the rise of Arab nationalism and later also due to policies of some Arab governments that sought to present the expulsion of Jews as a crowd-driven retaliatory act for the exodus of Arab refugees from Palestine.[22] Now, let's stop for a moment and see what some Arabs did to their Arab sisters and brothers (some of whom happened to be Jewish), who lived in safety within Arab countries, within Arab communities, and were citizens of Arab countries and neighbors in Arab lands. What did Arab governments do to the Jews? For the most part, Arab governments uprooted them and kicked them out. In fact, about one million Jews had to leave Arab lands involuntarily.[23] True, one must acknowledge that Zionist sympathizers among Arab Jews incited some Jews to leave Arab countries and not all Arabs approved of such treatment of the Jews. Still, Arab governments confiscated their places of worship, took away their communities and possessions and threw them out of Arab countries. This action by Arab governments in the 1950s and 1960s is contrary to the commandments of Allah and his messenger in the Holy Qur'an.

The loss of the Jewish population was keenly felt by many Muslims. My own family has stories of how Jews helped Muslims in Egypt during Ramadan, our month long day time fast. Jewish women would cook for their Muslim neighbors, as those fasting would take a much needed afternoon rest. This show of tangible support from their Jewish acquaintances gave them encouragement to complete the fast as they looked forward to a prepared meal after sundown. In addition, many Egyptian families acted as baby sitters for Jewish families on Yom Kippur, to allow Jewish parents to spend uninterrupted time at the synagogues in worship on Yom Kippur. This was also the case, not only in Egypt, but next door in the Holy Land as well.[24]

To spell it out clearly—Ahlul Kitab actually assisted each other in keeping their respective *Sharia*, united by one *Deen*.

Many Egyptians I know miss their former Jewish neighbors and were sorry to see them go. I am told by an old friend, Mr. Abdel Hady el Karamani, that he will never forget a story recounted by his father Mohamed where a Jewish jeweler in Cairo entrusted him with a very expensive diamond ring to show to his fiancée.

My uncle Mohamed el Gindy, who was in the leather goods trade business in old Cairo, often praised the integrity of his Jewish suppliers, traders and customers.

One may attempt to excuse the expulsion of the Jews by stating that Arab governments were still influenced by colonial powers, and Zionism was on the rise at that time.[25] Now, one is not saying that all the affected Arab Jews were angels. Some may have indeed betrayed their countries and spied for Israel, as has been claimed.

But the wrong-doers could have been dealt with separately.[26] Indeed, the Prophet Muhammad warned believers against collective punishment for the sins of a few, and he warned against the cry of the oppressed.[27] The renowned Muslim scholar Taqi ad-Din Ahmad ibn Taymiyyah (d. 1328) echoed the same notion when he declared that "The just nation prevails even if ruled by non-Muslim while the oppressor nation vanishes, even if ruled by Muslims."[28]

The Hebrew Bible also warns against collective punishment.[29] Therefore, any collective punishment employed by the Arab governments against Arab Jews is a transgression against God. And any collective punishment employed by Israel against Holy Land Arabs is also a transgression against God.

Both sides claim that they are the rightful descendants of Abraham. Both sides claim that God gave them the land; yet, both sides are transgressing against the same God who gave them the land. That is why peace is lost in the Holy Land.

Given the treatment of Arab Jews described above, couldn't one imagine that an acknowledgment by Arab governments that they unjustly expelled the Jews would soften the hearts of people on both sides of the conflict over the Holy Land? Then, going further, Arab governments could astound everyone by making an unconditional invitation to those Jews who were mistreated and eased out, even those who left voluntarily, to return to their communities and synagogues in Arab lands as protected people and not as an oppressed minority, as equal citizens of the land, not as second or third-class citizens.

Such a move would encourage the government of Israel to reciprocate and treat the Holy Land Arabs who live and work in Israel, not as second class citizens, but as equal citizens of the land. Why? The law of reciprocity is an integral part of the Bible.[30]

The notion of welcoming back Arab Jews into Arab land while the State of Israel occupies the Holy Land may be viewed by some Arabs as a bad idea. It may be viewed as "having it both ways". One reason for this view is that the Shas political party, founded by Arab Jews, is regarded by many members of the Arab community as an oppressor of the Holy Land Arabs. Therefore, how could one welcome the oppressors of fellow Arabs back into Arab Lands?

One could argue however that it is in the best interests of both the State of Israel and Arab governments to explore such an option. On the Jewish side there are three factors which detract from such options. First, the standard of living of the Jews in Israel is higher than it was in their former countries. In fact, it is often said that many Holy Land Arabs would prefer to live in the State of Israel than in a sovereign Palestinian state.[31] While that may be true, some Jews would rather live in the country of their ancestors. Some Jews also have a troubled conscience because of the way Holy Land Arabs are treated in the State of Israel and they would rather go to a country where everyone is treated equally.[32] After all, money is not everything. The Tanakh teaches that better is a little income with righteousness than great income with injustice.[33] Arab Jews may reason that it makes perfect sense to move to say Egypt or Morocco and have trade links between Israel and those states. There are flourishing Jewish communities in the Unites States, there is no reason there cannot be such communities again in Arab and Muslim countries.

Chief Rabbi Jonathan Sacks of Great Britain states that each one of us has something that someone else needs, and each one of us needs something someone else has, so we gain by interaction [and we lose by conflict]. Such interaction is what makes trade the most compelling counterforce to conflict.[34]

Secondly, one of the fears in the Jewish community is assimilation. As to the assimilation of Jews into Arab society, there is no more need to be concerned about that than assimilation anywhere else.

Islam forbids the marriage of a Muslim woman and Jewish man, so Islam has some built-in protection against assimilation. In the state of Israel, Jewish women have married Muslim men, so residing in Israel is no guarantee against interfaith marriage.[35]

While some Jews might see that living in close proximity with each other in the State of Israel gives them hope of a resurrected national identity, it is also important to realize that it is not wise to put all one's eggs in one basket. Jews residing in their ancestors' communities in Arab countries will foster mutual trust and build channels of trade between the State of Israel and those Arab regions. The return of Jews to Arab lands would be a trust-building step that is consistent with the Holy Qur'an message.[36] There is much precedence in history of building trust between Muslims and non-Muslims by giving equal status to dhimmi subjects in Muslim majority states,[37] starting with the Medina Charter of the Prophet Muhammad,[38] the Ott Katti Sharif reform of the Ottoman Empire,[39] and the Montefiore Edict of Toleration in Morocco.[40] Why would this be good for everyone? It would show that Arab governments have the confidence to face the truths of the past without fear. It would give Arab peoples a clear conscience and make them feel good that they stand on high moral ground.

Thirdly, the return of Arab Jews to Arab Lands may be viewed negatively by some Zionists. Why? Some would like to create a Jewish, ethnically pure, area in Palestine and are spending considerable resources to attract Jews to come to the Holy Land and live there permanently. Therefore, the main objection to the return of Arab Jews to Arab lands may be, not the Arab governments, but some Zionists.

---

1 - Heykal Pasha, *Official Records of The Second Session of The General Assembly, Ad Hoc Committee on the Palestinian Question, Summary Record of Meetings,* United Nations, 25 September to 25 November 1947, Lake Success, New York, Page 185. As quoted by, Ya'Akov Meron, *The Forgotten Millions: The Modern Jewish Exodus from Arab Lands,* (New York: Continuum, 1999) Page 84.

2 - Ibid page 83.

3 - H. J. Cohn, the Jews of The Middle east, 1860-1972, (Jerusalem: Israel University Press, 1973) page 67

4 - Ibid page 64

5 - Arthur Benveniste , "500th Anniversary of the Forced Conversion of the Jews of Portugal", From an address at Sephardic Temple Tifereth Israel, Los Angeles, October 1997

6 - Ibid page 86.
7 - Ibid pages 86 - 93
8 - Please see Exhibit 3, titled "Ethnic Cleansing."
9 - "In 1939, there were 17 million Jews in the world, and by 1945 only 11 million. "Ner Le Elef, World Jewish Population. http://simpletoremember.com/vitals/world-jewish-population.htm#_ftn1
10 - Allah said: **"Allah (swt) did aforetime take a covenant with the Children of Israel; and We raised up from among them twelve chieftains. And Allah (swt) said, 'I am with you. Surely, if you perform the prayer, and pay the alms, and believe in My Messengers, honour and assist them, and loan to Allah a beautiful loan, verily I will wipe out from you your evils, and admit you to gardens with rivers flowing beneath; but if any of you, after this, resisteth faith, he hath truly wandered from the path of rectitude. But because of their breach of their covenant, We cursed them, and made their hearts grow hard; they change the words from their (right) places and forget a good part of the message that was sent them, nor wilt thou cease to find them ever bent on (new) deceits, except a few of them. Yet pardon them, and forgive; surely Allah (swt) loves the good-doers".** (al-Maeda 5,12-16)
11 - James Carroll, Constantine's Sword: The Church and the Jews (New York, Houghton Mifflin Company, 2001) p 6.
12 - Omer Salem, Notes From the Quad, an alumni e-Magazine Yale Divinity School, in the summer of 2011. http://www.yale.edu/divinity/notes/110801/kiev
13 - David D. Freedman, "Legal Systems Very Different From Our Own", May 18, 2006
14 - Benjamin Abrahamson, Israel, via email dated May 15, 2012.
15 - **"If a non-Muslim asks you for asylum, grant it to him, so that he may hear the word of Allah. Then escort him to where he will be secure."** Qur'an 9:6. Speech at Tikkun conference: https://www.academia.edu/3307876/speech_in_Jerusalem
16 - "The armed resistance and the armed struggle are the path and the strategic choice for liberating the Palestinian land, from the [Mediterranean] sea to the [Jordan] river, and for the expulsion of the invaders and usurpers [Israel] . . . We won't relinquish one inch of the land of Palestine." Hamas leader in the Gaza Strip Ismail Haniyeh, The Western Center for Journalism, December 28, 2011
17 - Jimmy Carter, "Don't Give Up on Mideast Peace", New York Times, April 12,
18 - Bob Anschuetz, "Let's End Our Wars on the "Other": U.S. Interests, Israeli Fears, and the Demonization of Iran", Tikkun Magazine: To heal, repair and transform the world, January 2, 2012.
19 - Ellen Lust, the Middle East (Washington DC: CQ Press, 2011) page 460.
20 - James Carroll, Constantine's Sword: The Church and the Jews (New York, Houghton Mifflin Company, 2001) p 5.
21 - Prof. Ada Aharoni , The Forced Migration of Jews from Arab Countries and Peace, The Ben Gurion University in Beersheba, Dept of Education, 7.5.2004
23 - Malka Hillel Shulewitz, The Forgotten Millions: The Modern Jewish Exodus from Arab Lands, (London: Continuum 2001).
24 - "Zionism is a form of nationalism for Jews and Jewish culture . . . [that] support Jews upholding their Jewish identity and opposes the assimilation of Jews into other societies and has advocated the return of Jews to The State of Israel as a means for Jews to be liberated from anti-Semitic discrimination, exclusion, and persecution that has occurred in other societies." Werner Bergmann, Rainer Erb, Belinda Cooper, "Anti-Semitism in Germany", (New Jersey: Transaction Publishers, 1997)
25 - Rabbi Yisroel Dovid Weiss, "Muslim families babysat Jewish children on Yom Kippur before 1948." https://www.youtube.com/watch?v=Wpc2mpGDZrk

26 - Imam Nawawi, Ryadul Saleheen (Cairo: Hadith Publications, 2009) 67. "Be careful of the prayer of the oppressed. Even if the oppressed is not a Muslim, his prayer will be answered in this life and he will be judged about his faith in the next life."
27 - Ibn Taymihhah, fatawi Ibn Taymyyah, (2001: Cairo Press volume 4, page 26.)
28 - **Deuteronomy 24:16 Parents are not to be put to death for their children, nor children put to death for their parents; each will die for their own sin."**
29 - According to Professor Ya'akov Meron, who ia an Expert in Islamic Law and has a vast knowledge of the Arab world, the [Jews] were expelled, Malka Hillel Shulewitz, "The Forgotten Millions: the Modern Jewish Exodus from Arab Land", (London: Continuum, 2000) page xvi.
30 - Whatever is disagreeable to yourself do not do unto others. (Shayast-na-Shayast 13:29)
31 - Daniel Pipers, "The Hell of Israel is Better then the Paradise of Arafat", Middle East Quarterly, Spring 2005, p 43.
32 - Occupation, Colonialism, Apartheid. "Democracy and Governance Program", Middle East Project May 2009.
33 - Proverb16:8
34 - Jonathan Sacks, *The Dignity of Difference* (London: Continuum Publishing, 2002) p. 15
35 - Aware that Judaism forbids interfaith marriage for both men and women, the author wishes to point out that the reason Islam permits a marriage between a Muslim man and Jewish woman is because it is assumed that the Muslim husband will allow his wife full religious freedom. Islamic societies could not make this assumption about Jewish or Christian men.
36 - Allah said: "If a non- Muslim asks you for asylum, grant it to him, so that he may hear the word of Allah. Then escort him to where he will be secure." Q9:6. وَإِنْ أَحَدٌ مِّنَ الْمُشْرِكِينَ اسْتَجَارَكَ فَأَجِرْهُ حَتَّى يَسْمَعَ كَلاَمَ اللهِ ثُمَّ أَبْلِغْهُ مَأْمَنَهُ
37 - *Dhimmi* is the Arabic name for non-Muslims living in Muslim-ruled land.
38 - A. Guillaume, *The Life of Muhammad — A Translation of Ishaq's Sirat Rasul Allah*, Oxford University Press, Karachi, 1955; pp. 231–233.
39 - Norman Stillman, The Jews of Arab Land (Philadelphia: The Jewish Publication Society, 1979) p 97. The Katt-i Sharif: enumeration of reforms that affected the individual subjects of the Ottoman Empire. It echoed many of the libertarian ideals that had been voiced in the French Declaration of the Rights of Man.
40 - Norman Stillman, Ibid., p 100. On February 5, 1864, Mawlay Muhammad issued a dahir, or royal decree, declaring his intention to treat his Jews with complete justice as was due any Moroccan subject and to protect them from all oppression.

THE MISSING PEACE
THE ROLE OF RELIGION IN THE **ARAB-ISRAELI** CONFLICT

HOLY LAND

What could happen if one respects the semantics that Allah uses in the Holy Qur'an? For example, Allah describes someone who is pious, prays, fasts, and gives to charity as a *believer* (Arabic: مؤمن Mo'amen). If one changed what Allah said and called that person *infidel* (Arabic: كافر Kafer), then one would be changing the word of Allah and, therefore, would not be faithful to the word of Allah.

By the same token, if Allah calls a certain location both in the Qur'an[1] and in the Torah[2] "the Holy Land"(Hebrew: ארץ הקודש ; Eretz HaQodesh. Arabic: A l - Ard Al Muqaddasah الأرض المقدسة), and one insists on calling it another name, such as the Land of Palestine, then one is changing the word of Allah. The question then is this: if the area between the Mediterranean Sea and the Dead Sea is called the Holy Land in the Qur'an, then why does anyone who is a follower of Muhammad call it Palestine? Where does the name Palestine come from? Is this an Arabic name? No. Is it in the Holy Qur'an? No. The word Palestine derives from the Greek "Palestina," translated into English as "Philistine." The word "philistine" as referring to a person has several derogatory meanings,[3] including "one regarded as a natural or traditional enemy because [of] belonging to a despised class" and as "a crass prosaic often priggish individual guided by material rather than intellectual values." Other meanings include "ignoramus," "outsider," and "one oblivious to aesthetics." Is it now understood why the West in general and the English-speaking world in particular do not look favorably on the name "philistine"? Philistine is a derogatory or pejorative term in English, just as *Kafer* is a derogatory or pejorative term in Arabic. Lets us thus cleave to "Holy Land", an acceptable term to Muslims, Jews, and Christians.[4]

If Arabs truly love Allah and respect and revere Allah's word, then they should reflect such love by using the name Allah gave in the Qur'an to the land commonly called Palestine, namely, they should call that land the Holy Land, *Al-Ard Al-Muqaddasah*, just as the name of the holy city to which the Prophet Muhammad immigrated was changed from Yathrib to Medina to fulfill Allah's command.[5] One should have no doubt that Allah will be pleased if one uses the names Allah gave in the Qur'an. Now, let's look at the word Israel or B'nai Israel. That word is mentioned forty-one times in the Holy Qur'an, and it is mentioned approximately 2,575 times in the Holy Bible.

The criteria here, however, should not be the number of times a word is mentioned but the context in which it is often mentioned. The word Philistine is associated with "uncircumcised" people (i.e., unholy or godless people), while the word Israel is associated with "circumcised" people or people of God. According to the King James Version of the Holy Bible, Israel is defined as one who prevails with God or one who let God prevail. Israel was a name given to the Prophet Jacob at Bethel. Israel is a name that applies to the Prophet Jacob's descendants and to their kingdom. According to the KJV, Israel means the true believer in Jesus Christ as explained by the Apostle Paul. The name of Israel is, therefore, variously used to denote 1) the Prophet Jacob, 2) the literal descendants of Jacob, and 3) the true believers in Jesus Christ, and according to Mormon doctrine, regardless of their lineage or geographical location.[6]

This is akin to the name "Sharif" or "Hashemite" in the Muslim tradition. The name Hashemite or Sharif is variously used to denote 1) the Prophet Muhammad, 2) the literal descendants of the Prophet Muhammad through his daughter Fatima, 3) the true believers in the Prophet Muhammad, regardless of their lineage or geographical location and 4) the modern Hashemite Kingdom of Jordan.

Now, Allah referred to Palestine as the Holy Land for a reason. The reason is to sanctify and purify the soul and spirit of those who visit the Holy Land. Because it is called the Holy Land, the proper mechanism to handle the Arab-Israeli conflict cannot be a secular institution but must be a religious institution with credible leadership, trusted by both sides, scholars who are considered God-fearing as well as knowledgeable about all three faiths.

One could think of the Holy Land as a hospital, a hospital for the heart so to speak, where a sick person goes to receive treatment. People flee to such a land when they have nowhere else to go, just as Muslims flee to the Holy Lands of Mecca and Medina when they feel that their spiritual life needs alignment or realignment. Pious Jews and Christians consider Jerusalem, where parts of the the Bible were revealed, and Hebron where Prophets and Patriarchs are buried, the Holy Land. This is parallel to Mecca where the Qur'an was revealed, and Medina where the Prophet and the Companions (Arabic: *Sahaba*) are buried, places which serve as a location to sanctify oneself.[7]

However, for some people, the illness is so severe that they want to stay in the hospital forever, and they would rather die in the hospital than die anywhere else. Also, some people choose to live in the hospital because they are afraid that if they leave the hospital, they will become sick - even die or be killed, just as Muslims yearn to travel to Mecca and Medina and live there and to die there and be buried there.

Jerusalem and Mecca

Although the role of Jerusalem in Islam is not as significant as Mecca is, Jerusalem is the center stage for all Muslim eschatological expectation. The centrality of Jerusalem to the Messianic hope of Jews, Christians and Muslims cannot be forgotten. This is why it is worthwhile to stress that the Jewish tradition of King Messiah and Islamic traditions of Al Mahdi (pbuh) will be fulfilled by one and the same person. It may be noted that some Haredi (ultra-orthodox) Jews believe that they must not jump ahead of God and the Messiah by returning to Israel and taking it over by force before the advent of the Messiah.

In March 2010, Sheikh Tantawi, the Grand Imam of Al Azhar Mosque, the largest Islamic theological Institute in the world, sensing his death to be imminent, travelled to Medina, where he died a few days later and was buried in Maqbaratu al-Baqī' (Arabic: Al-Baqi مقبرة البقيع Cemetery). Tantawi made the journey because an Islamic tradition holds that the best and purest place on earth is Al-Baqi' Cemetery. Likewise, some Christians and pious Jews yearn to travel to the Holy Land, some as mere religious tourists and some as pilgrims, to purify their hearts and cleanse their souls and follow in the footsteps of their prophets Abraham, Isaac, Jacob, David and Solomon.

While Jews experience physical freedom in the United States, the Holy Land is the only place on earth where a Jew feels both physical and spiritual freedom. Jews and Christians have a faith tradition originating in the Holy Land. The Holy Qur'an affirms that both the Jews and Christians can be referred to as B'nai Israel.[8] Both faith traditions have their Holy Books (the Tanakh in Hebrew and the Gospel in Greek) revealed completely or partially in the Holy Land.

Temple Mount

No talk about Jerusalem is complete until we discuss the Temple Mount, or *Haram al – Sharif.*

The Temple Mount is located in Jerusalem's Old City. In Hebrew it is called *"Har HaBáyit"* (mount of the house [of worship]), and *"Har HaMōriyā"* (mount Moriah). In Arabic it is referred to as the *Haram al-Sharif* (noble sanctuary), and is one of the most important religious sites in Jerusalem. The following are quotes from the Bible and the Qur'an referring to the Temple Mount:

> Then Solomon began to build the Temple of the Lord in Jerusalem on Mount Moriah. It was on the threshing-floor of Araunah the Jebusite, the place provided by David, his father." - 2 Chronicles 3:1

> "Glory be to Him who did take His servant for a Journey by night from the Sacred Sanctuary to the farthest Sanctuary, whose precincts We did bless . . . " - The Qur'an, Sura Al-Isra' 17:1"

The Temple Mount is important to Muslims because it was the first *qibla* (destination of prayer) before Allah ordered prophet Muhammad to change the *qibla* from *Masjid Aqsa* (the al Aska Mosque located on the Temple Mount) to *Masjid Haram* (the shrine in Mecca). The Qur'an records the change in *qibla*, and refers those who object to such change as "the fools"; here is the Quranic text:

> "The fools among the people will say: "What hath turned them from the *Qibla* to which they were used?" Say: To Allah belong both east and West: Allah guides whom Allah wills to a Way that is straight" (Q2:142)

Then Allah clarified to Prophet Muhammad unequivocally in the Holy Qur'an that Allah wishes Ahlul Qur'an (Muslims) to have a one *qibla* – *Masjid Haram* in Mecca - and that Ahlul Kitab (Jews) have a separate *qibla* – The Temple Mount, Jerusalem. Here is the proof text for the two different *qiblas*:

> "And even if you bring to those who have been given the Book every sign they would not follow your *qibla*, nor can you be a follower of their *qibla*, neither are they the followers of each other's *qibla*, and if you follow their desires after the knowledge that has come to you, then you shall most surely be among the unjust." (Q2:145)

If there was one verse in the Holy Quran that gives God-fearing Jews the right to pray on the Temple Mount, or to share the Temple Mount with their Muslim neighbors, this verse is it.

However, the author joins his voice to the many voices of Rabbis inside and outside the Holy Land in advising God-fearing Jews not to force their way on the Temple Mount against the wishes of the Muslims in the Holy Land. On this matter, patience is golden. With the help of almighty God, there will rise a group of Muslim and Jewish scholars (Imams and Rabbis) who will agree on how and when the Jews are to pray in peace on the Temple Mount. Jews have waited two millennium for such an honor, no harm will befall the Jewish people if they reach out to Muslim scholars and wait a little. It is worth mentioning here that some pious Jews are quite concerned, disturbed, jealous and may be angry that some Palestinian youth are permitted and could play soccer on the Temple Mount, while pious Jews are not allowed to worship G-d on the Temple mount.

Why do we dispute the Qibla of Ahlul Kitab?[9] If Allah and His beloved prophet affirmed the right of Ahlul Kitab to Jerusalem, why do we deny them such right?[10]

Do we Muslims know that denying Ahlul Kitab their right to Jerusalem has caused Allah to punish us? Allah has penalized us by having Ahlul Kitab deny our Hajj route from Egypt to Mecca through the Negev desert! Muslims in North Africa can no longer perform Hajj the same way our ancestors did - over land. Our Hajj route has been blocked by Israel, which denies access without prior permission. Furthermore, if Israel grants permission for Muslims to perform Hajj by passing through the Negev, the Kingdom of Saudi Arabia will deny us access to Mecca because we passed through Israel!

As Muslims we know that Mecca is two hundred times more important to Allah than Jerusalem is. Where did we come up with this ratio? In the hadith of Prophet Muhammad: "Prayer at the Haram Mosque hundred thousand prayers, prayers in the mosques of Madinah a thousand prayers, prayers in Jerusalem five hundred prayers."[11]

Furthermore, a study of all Muslim centers of learnings and jurisprudence was performed comparing Jerusalem to Mecca, Madinah, Karbala, Basra, Cairo, Damascus, Khorasan, Fez and other Islamic centers of learnings. In the study, Jerusalem appear at the bottom of Muslim cities producing ulama (scholars), fuqaha (jurists) and qudah (judges).[12] Therefore, as an Islamic scholar, I attest that given the above facts, the Negev is much more important to the Muslim *ummah* than Jerusalem is.

---

1 - Ibidem Qur'an 5: 21 "O my people! enter the holy land which Allah has prescribed for you and turn not on your backs for then you will turn back losers."
2 - The Harper Collins Study Bible, Exodus 3:5 (New York: HarperCollins Publishers, 2006) 88.
3 - Philip Grove, Webster Third New International Dictionary, Unabridged (Sringfield, MA: Mariam-Webster Inc. Publishers, 1993) pp 1697
4 - To test my theory about calling Philistine the Holy Land among Arabs, a visit was made to the local Mosque on George Street in New Haven, CT, Masjdul Islam, where. Shaikh Imadudeen Abu Hijleh from Palestine was there. I asked him if he would mind that we call Philistine the Holy Land instead, he had some resistance first, and then he said "there is nothing wrong with using a Qur'anic name. I am only looking for justice and dignity for my family in the Holy Land and outside the Holy Land" I told him glad tidings, this will happen. Insh'Allah
5 - Qur'an 9:120
6 - KJV, The Holy Bible (Salt Lake City: Published by the LDS Church, 1979) p. 708.
7 - Just as Shia consider Qum in Iran and Najaf in Iraq as Holy Lands; as Hindu Indians consider Kashi Vishwanath in Benaras, UP, a Holy Land; Sikhs consider Amritsar in the Punjab Holy Land.; and Catholics consider the Vatican Holy Land. See link for more holy places around the world. http://en.wikipedia.org/wiki/List_of_religious_sites#Bah.C3.A1.27.C3.AD_Faith

8 - "Then a portion of the Children of Israel believed, and a portion disbelieved: But we gave power to those who believed, against their enemies, and they became the ones that prevailed." Qur'an 61:14
9 - Gamal abdel Hady and Wafa Refaat, Jews Have No right to Palestine, El Wafa press, El Mansoura, 1981.
10 - Qura'n 2:145 and 17:1.
11 - Tabarani in the Mogam al Kabeer, page 432
12 - Yakut's "the Dictionary of Learned men"; Oleg Grabar, The Encyclopedia of Islam, "Al-Kuds," (Leiden: E.J. Brill, 1980) page 322 to page 333; Clifford E. Bosworth, The New Islamic Dynasties, (Edinburgh: Edinburgh Press, 2004)

THE MISSING PEACE
THE ROLE OF RELIGION IN THE **ARAB-ISRAELI** CONFLICT

section two

Top 10 Objections
to repatriation

THE MISSING PEACE
THE ROLE OF RELIGION IN THE **ARAB-ISRAELI** CONFLICT

TOP 10 OBJECTIONS
TO REPATRIATION

Generally speaking, Arab politicians do not have a problem with the repatriation of Arab Jews.[1] It is Arab religious leaders that need to be convinced - using the Holy Qur'an - of the value of such repatriation. The challenges religious leaders may face are with the radical Muslim groups and the way they exegete the Holy Qur'an to say that Jews are infidels and therefore should prevent the Jews from returning to Arab lands. They also disapprove of Jews having a homeland in Palestine.[2]

The following section delineates the top-ten religious and non-religious objections leveled by powerful Arab clerics to Jews' returning to and reclaiming their communities in Arab countries.[3] Included here as well are Qur'anic answers to those objections, which are often concealed deliberately from the masses or misquoted to keep the conflict alive. The conflict allows certain Arab regimes to hold on to power and justify anti-Semitism.

1. Jewish and Arab Enmity

Excerpt from a lecture to graduates at the
College of Languages and Translation, Al Azhar University,
Cairo, Egypt, 2012

First objection: someone might say, but the Qur'an says the Jews are the enemies of the believers;[4] the Jews killed Allah's prophets.[5] How can someone ask us to allow the enemies of Allah to return to the land?[6] Are you out of your mind?

There are two points to make here: firstly, if the Jews killed the prophets of Allah, where did those prophets of Allah go after they were killed? If they were false prophets, then they were misleading the people and they received their punishment as commanded in the Holy Qur'an and the Torah.[7] However, if those were true prophets of Allah, then according to the Holy Qur'an they went to heaven.[8]

In addition, Allah told us in the Holy Qur'an to treat our enemies with *Ihsan,* which is to say with kindness, integrity, and respect (dignitism).[9] And Allah said: kindness will be met with kindness, integrity will be met with integrity and respect will be met with respect.[10] And even if Arabs hate the Jews because of some narrative Arabs have heard or read, or because of sixty years of bitter history, Allah warns the believers against failing to treat a person with integrity, even if one hates that person.[11] According to the Qur'an,[12] the Jews, like any other people, can be the best people who have ever lived, or they can be the worst.[13]

Allah said that the Jews will be with us to the end of time.[14] If Muslim or Christian religious leaders think that the Jews will abandon Judaism and convert to Christianity or Islam, they are deluding themselves and they will be disappointed.

Benzion Netanyahu, the late father of the current Israeli Prime Minster, argued that the *conversos*—the Jews who converted to Christianity in Spain— were killed by the thousands for allegedly practicing Judaism in secret. Netanyahu stated that those Jews were actually practicing Christianity. The Spaniards' extermination of those Jews came from a deep anti-Semitism, not from religious persecution.[15] Netanyahu is clearly advising his fellow Jews that even conversion will not save you from the sword - hence, stand fast as a Jew, do not convert. Therefore, it is good to know how to accept the Jews for what they are, not for what a Muslim or a Christian religious leader wishes they were. It is good to bring out the best in a Jew and avoid the worst.[16]

Dignitism as a path to peace

Now, there are ways to encourage the Jews to become good neighbors, and there are ways to ensure that they will be our worst enemies. Arab governments do not lose anything by helping the Jews become the best neighbors. One can achieve this by treating the Jews with ihsan, which is respect, kindness, charity and integrity. Therefore, dignitism is the practice of treating all people according to their God-given dignity, i.e. treating them with respect, kindness, and integrity. Dignitism is a new civilization paradigm aimed to place the human in sync with 'Divinity.'[17] If Arabs treat the Jews with dignitism, Allah may put in their hearts the impetus to forgive the wrongs perpetrated on them. If the Jews forgive and ask forgiveness, they will be the best human beings that have ever lived. Why? The Jews have a long history of persecution and subjugation to forgive—more than do Christians or Muslims. Moreover, when one hates and treats people with dishonor or disrespect, one inevitably bring out the worst in those people, regardless of their chosen religious tradition.

In the Qur'an, Allah says, **"Ihsan will be met with Ihsan."** If one says yes, we will do Ihsan, but not with the Jews, then one is changing the word of Allah. Allah wants Muslims to practice, perform, and implement Ihsan with everyone, Muslim and non-Muslim. [18]

As I declared in my speech at the Tikkun conference, Jerusalem, in 2012, the Qur'an teaches that Allah created all people, tongues, tribes, and nations, and Allah made all His creation dignified.[19] Just like the children of Israel have intrinsic dignity, the children of Ishmael have intrinsic dignity. As it says in the Qur'an,

We have dignified and honored the children of Adam (17:70)

Allah did not say, We have honored the Hasidim or Haredim or Salafi or Sufi. No, all people are honored: female and male, black and white, children of Ismael and children of Israel are honored.

Muslims also guilty of killing Sahaba and Awlia

Secondly, we Arabs and Muslims are guilty of the same offense we accuse our Jewish brothers and sisters of, namely, the killing of prophets. Why? The prophet Muhammad is reported to have said: "the learned *ulama* (scholars) of my *ummah* (people) are akin to the prophets of B'nai Israel."[20] In that Hadith, the ulama of the Islamic nation are the equivalent of the prophets of B'nai Israel. That being the case, history tells us that we Muslims have killed many *ulama*, *awlia* and *khulafa* (caliphs, leaders) including some of the greatest heirs to the Prophet Muhammad such as Omar Ibnul Khattab,

Othman Ibn Affan, Talha, Zubair, Ali Ibn Abi Taleb, Al Hussain Ibn Ali, Al Hassan Ibn Ali and many others. This must give Muslims pause when accusing Jews of the same deed.

2. Jews as neighbors

Second objection: someone might say, "How can we have Jews as our neighbors, in the same town? Did not the Prophet Muhammad drive the Jews out of Medina?" Well, the Prophet Muhammad may have expelled some people who were accused of wrongdoing, irrespective of their faith.[21]

However, he accepted Jews as his neighbors in Medina and was married to a Jewish woman, the mother of the believers: *Safiyyah bint Huyayy*,[22] furthermore; a Jew named Avi Shachm in Medina kept Muhammad's shield in trust.[23] According to John Esposito, the Prophet Muhammad himself engaged in dialogue with the Christians of Najran, resulting in a mutually agreeable relationship whereby the Najranis were permitted to pray in the Prophet's Mosque in Medina.[24] In 644, it is narrated that the Muslim Caliph 'Umar ibn al-Khattab (RA) brought seventy Jewish families back to Jerusalem after the Jews had been expelled from the Holy Land under Byzantine Christian rule.[25] In 1187, when the Muslim sultan and warrior Saladin conquered Jerusalem and took it from the crusaders, he brought back the Jews who had been banned by Christian rulers from living or worshipping in Jerusalem.[26] Also, during the Muslim rule of Spain (750 AD to 1250 AD) interfaith harmony was at exemplary levels. *Convivencia* (living together) in respect and honor prevailed in Spain among Muslims, Christians and Jews.

Such honor and mutual respect reached levels which appear to be outstanding compared to today's Middle East. For example: Samuel Ha-Levi (d. 1056), later known as Samuel Ha-Nagid ("the prince"), was the political head of the Jews of Granada in the 11th Century. Ha-Levi quickly rose through the notable ranks to the position of vizier and councilor to the King. When King Habbus died, his son King Muzafar Nasir, who also favored Ha-Levi replaced him. In addition to his position as vizier, Ha-Levi was appointed commander of the King's Muslim armies. Samuel and his son, Joseph, were given command over the Muslim army. Ha-Levi led the Muslim army in eighteen years of warfare and was killed on the battlefield.[27]

3. Can Jews and Christians accept Muslims?

Third objection: someone else might say, but Allah said that Jews and Christians would never be satisfied with the Prophet Muhammad, no matter what the Prophet Muhammad might do for them, unless he follows their cult.[28] Yes, you are right, Allah said that neither the Jews nor the Christians will be happy with the Prophet Muhammad until he follows the precepts of their culture, therefore it is written, **"O' Muhammad, do not seek their satisfaction. O' Muhammad, only seek the satisfaction of Allah."**

The logic is that if you follow the precepts of the Jews, the Christians will be unhappy with you, and if you follow the precepts of the Christians, the Jews will be unhappy with you. For example, to satisfy the Jews, you have to reject Jesus Christ as God and the Trinity, which are central to Christian belief, and to satisfy Christians, you have to uphold the Trinity and the deity of Jesus Christ, which are unacceptable to Jews. Therefore, it was said to Muhammad that you can never simultaneously satisfy both Jews and Christians—doing so is impossible. Just be a Muslim the way the Patriarch Abraham taught, and let Jews be Jews and Christians be Christians. Only seek the satisfaction and acceptance of Allah by inviting Jews and Christians to follow the truth that was revealed to you, or invite the Jews and Christians to follow the truth that was revealed to them.[29]

A key distinction to highlight here is the difference between *Deen* (basic religion) and *Shari'a* (covenant). There is One Religion, which is obligated upon all mankind, Jews call it B'nai Noah, Christians call it Natural Law, and Muslims call it both *Deen* and "Islam" when this term is used in its broader sense. The Muslim judge, Qatada ibn al-Nu'man (d. 720) said *"al-din wahid wa al-Shari'a mukhtalifah"* (religion is one, *shari'a* is diverse).[30] This is taught throughout the Qur'an and Hadith, and it was made into a political reality by the Ottoman Empire.

4. The Return of all refugees

Fourth objection: someone might say, "But what about the Palestinians? Shouldn't Arab governments ask The state of Israel to allow the Palestinians to go back to the Holy Land in exchange for our allowing the Jews to come back to Arab land?" Of course, one could ask for anything one wants as a condition for accepting the Arab Jews back; however, one would be wiser to postpone such a condition. Why? Because the Jews, with all their weapons and military arsenal, are still fearful and feel unsafe. Someone might call that paranoia, but to the Jews in the Holy Land it is not paranoia, it is real fear. They wake up each morning with a view of Arab guns and rockets surrounding them and enemies wanting them out of the Holy Land.

Therefore, one could postpone such a request for several years after the return of the Jews to their communities and synagogues in Arab lands. When the Jews feel safe, secure, and reconciled in their homes and communities in Arab Lands, one could argue that the Jewish people and the international community will invite the Holy Land Arabs of the Diaspora, who wish to go back to the Holy Land, to return home. Why? It makes good political and economic sense and helps heal the wounds inflicted on the Holy Land Arabs! Also, the Israelis need to stimulate their economy and to show the world that they can live up to the commandment of reciprocity in the Torah.[31]

For now, the Jews fear being outnumbered completely by their current Holy Land Arab residents. They are concerned that the Arabs would vote to treat them as second-class citizens or expel them from the Holy Land. In effect, Israelis fear that the Holy Land Arabs may treat them the same way Holy Land Arabs in the West Bank are getting treated today. That is why it is important to heed the golden rule – do not do unto others what you would not have them do unto you.

In short, the Jews are afraid of what is commonly known in the State of Israel as "the genetic time bomb" - Arab women bearing more children than Jewish women. So one must first assure that the minority Jews in Arab Land are safe and equal citizens. This mutual trust is a real possibility and supported by the Holy Qur'an.[32] As the Dean of Religious life at Stanford University said, ". . . building trust across [religious] divides can change [for the better] the way potential leaders think, feel and lead."[33] Moreover, once we view ourselves as coreligionists, sharing one *Deen* and different *Sharia*, the fear of "demographic threat" is sure to fade.

It is possible to think backwards in time in terms of reciprocal expatriation. It is also possible to think forward in time in terms of open borders and European Union style commonwealth. The key is finding a sufficient common regional history. Someone wrote to the Turkish Islamic creationist, Adnan Oktar, and said *"As-salamun alaykom* my Master Mohammad Adnan. Our expectation from you in this period [after the 2010 Gaza flotilla incident] is to make a fiercer statement regarding Israel, *Insha'Allah."*

Oktar replied, "You want a fierce statement? Let us not do that but show compassion to these people. Why don't you try this, instead? The entire world hates Jews. Do not do this; that is a sin that is a transgression. There is no need for such bitterness in one's standpoint. As Muslims, let us show compassion, let us watch over the Jews and protect them, then these people would relax. Of course their full obedience to the concept of Mahdi is a necessity. Otherwise they would be waging a war against the Torah . . . They are praying day and night saying "O Lord, send us the Messiah"; they are praying night and day saying "Moshiach, Moshiach"[34]

5. Who May Finance repatriation

Fifth objection: someone might ask, "Where is the money going to come from to restore all the synagogues and communities, so that they are sound and functional for Jews to return?" The best choice would be for a joint Arab-Jewish effort to rebuild those communities and synagogues in their land.

Allah will help the Arabs because they are performing a good deed for other people. In addition, many wealthy Jews will probably be glad to rebuild damaged Jewish synagogues and communities in Arab lands if Arab governments let them. Arab governments would then have loyal and productive citizens for their society. They can offer citizenship to Palestinians as Jews return to Arab lands.

Arab governments may allocate part of their military spending to build communities and places of worship, which would be far less costly than buying weapons to fight Israel.

6. The claim that Zionism does not support peace

Sixth objection: someone might say, but the State of Israel does not want peace. The Zionists came to Palestine in order to demolish the Muslim Shrine in Jerusalem and build the Third Temple. The Jews came to destroy the religion of Islam.

Well, the facts appear to be contrary to that claim. The State of Israel has given back land equivalent to three times its size to achieve peace with Egypt—the Sinai Peninsula. The State of Israel signed peace treaties with Egypt and Jordan and was willing to return the Golan Heights in exchange for peace with Syria. Also, the prisoner exchange history between the state of Israel and its neighbors may also refute the above claim. To illustrate this point, four examples are provided: First, in 1967, seventeen Israeli soldiers were exchanged for 4,238 Egyptian soldiers, 553 Jordanian soldiers, and 367 Syrian soldiers held captive.[35] Second, in 1983 six Israeli soldiers were exchanged for 4,765 Palestinians and Lebanese imprisoned at Ansar camp.[36] Third, in May 1985, three Israeli soldiers were released in exchange for 1,150 Palestinian prisoners and detainees in Israeli jails, during the "Jibril deal".[37] Fourth, in 2011, the Israeli soldier Gilad Shalit was exchanged for 1,027 Palestinian prisoners, including some convicted of multiple murders and carrying out terror attacks against Israeli civilians.[38] The above numbers show an average prisoner exchange rate of one to 623. On these matters, numbers speak louder than rhetoric.

As to the claim that Jews came to the Holy Land to destroy the religion of Islam by demolishing the Muslim shrine in Jerusalem and replacing it with the Third Temple, this claim can also be refuted. For, how could a religion, protected by Allah, be destroyed by the demolition of a building, even if that building is the shrine in Jerusalem or the Kaaba in Mecca? The Kaaba was destroyed two times by humans and seven times by natural causes, yet Islam was not destroyed.[39] While some radical Zionists may wish for the demolition of the Muslim shrine on the Temple mount to clear way for the Third Jewish Temple, cooler heads often prevail on this issue.[40] Jews are perfectly aware that destroying the Muslim shrine in Jerusalem would ignite the wrath of Muslims around the globe. The Jews would be at war with the very people who saved the Jews from destruction by the Christians during the Crusades.

Indeed, Haredi rabbis repeatedly announce that it is forbidden for Jews to ascend the area of the Temple Mount until the Moshiach arrives for two reasons. First, because there are areas there that are so sacred that no Jew can tread there until the purification process that can only be performed in the rebuilt Temple, and that camp holds that the Temple will not be rebuilt until Moshiach arrives. Second, Haredi Rabbis hold that it is forbidden to provoke the nations of the world. So an entire segment of the Jewish people cannot even go to the area of the Temple Mount, let alone do any damage there![41]

Rabbis endowed with good judgment and common sense know that challenging the Muslims on the Temple Mount is not in the best interest of the Jews, and they advise their followers not to engage Muslims on this issue. It is fair to say, however, that the Temple Mount is sufficiently large, spanning thirty-six acres, and there is enough room for Jews and Muslims to worship on the Temple Mount. If pious Jews so desire, pious Muslims could help them in their endeavor to build a Temple to replace Herod's Temple in Jerusalem. If pious Muslims are involved in the planning and building of the Third Temple, the Third Temple will last for more years than if the Muslims were challenged, ridiculed and their Jerusalem shrine destroyed.

7. Aggression rewarded

Seventh objection: Someone might say, if Arab governments agree to peace with the State of Israel, they will be acknowledging defeat, in effect rewarding Israeli aggression. Are you asking Arab governments to concede defeat to Israel - cknowledge losing to the Zionist enemy?

In all its wars, the State of Israel claims to have acted in self-defense. Israel states that ever since the partition plan of 1947, Jews wanted a place to call home and to live in peace with their neighbors.

The Jewish people look forward to trade with their neighbors far more eagerly than they do to war. Therefore, agreeing to peace, implementing Islamic moral values, resolving the humanitarian crisis of the refugees and applying Qur'anic principles is a sign of courage, not of defeat.

With open peace between Arabs and Jews, Arab governments will be conceding defeat, not to Israel, but to bigotry and hate. That is the right kind of defeat to have. Even if Arabs lose this battle to the State of Israel, Arabs will be winning the moral war against stubbornness and dogmatism.

8. Some Jews may refuse repatriation

Eighth objection: what if the Jews refuse to come back to reclaim their synagogues and their communities? First of all, since many Jews love their countries of origin, one would doubt that as a whole the Jewish people will refuse to come back to the land of their ancestors. It is safe to say that, if the Jews are offered such opportunity and the offer is genuine, many of them would take it. Many Jews say that, while their bodies exist outside their native country, their hearts yearn to return to the land of their forefathers in North Africa, Egypt, Iraq, Persia, the Levant and Yemen.

Secondly, even if the Jews do not take the offer of return, the Arabs would have done the right thing. The Arabs would have proved that they can face truth with confidence in God and a clear conscience. Allah will be the Arabs' witness that they did what is right in the sight of Allah.

Doing good in the sight of Allah and having the right belief go hand in hand in Islam. In fact, doing good in practice is the proof of having the right belief in the heart. This is why the Holy Qur'an speaks of true Muslims very often as "those who believe and do good deeds". Both the Qur'an and the Holy Prophet have told Muslims that the best among them is that person who shows the best behavior towards other people. In the fourth chapter of the Qur'an, Allah commands the Muslim people by saying:

> **"Be maintainers of justice and bearers of true witness for Allah, even if it (the truth) goes against your own**

selves or parents or relatives or someone who is rich or poor." (Qur'an 4:135)

9. Concessions with nothing in return

Ninth objection: someone might say, "This looks like another Zionist ploy to cause Arab governments to make more concessions for which Arabs get nothing in return." One could argue that this is not a ploy. Why? It is a well-known fact that some members of the Zionist camp would like to bring all the Jews in the world to the Holy Land. The extreme among them want to demolish the Muslim shrine on the Temple mount and replace it with the Third Temple as described in the biblical book of Ezekiel.[42] Such an event will most likely lead to conflict and bloodshed, but they are willing to take the risk. Some fringe elements do not want any Jew to leave the Holy Land and return to the country he or she came from. They would like to make the Holy Land an ethnically pure area for the Jews.

Israel offers plane tickets, citizenship, no-interest loans, free language classes, rental assistance or free housing, jobs, discounts in purchasing cars, child allowance, *a move-in bonus* of up to US $20,000 to Jews so that the Jews could leave their country and come to live permanently in the Holy Land. If Arabs look upon this with dismay, then I again declare here as I did in my speech in Cairo, 2012, that Arabs should consider giving the Jews the right of return to their Arab lands. Why? Such a plan will take an arrow out of those Zionists' quiver. Some hold Arabs and Muslims in low esteem; they do not think that Arabs will ever have the moral courage to consider correcting past inequities. They think that there is no place in Muslim-Arab hearts for non-Muslims. Coming out with such a plan will show that they were wrong in thinking about Arabs that way. The good in Islam and in the Arab world will thus be revealed for all to see.

Some Muslim Imams may think that the presence of Jews in the Holy Land as a sovereign nation dents their pride and indirectly challenges the superiority of Allah's final messenger. Those Imams should pause and think about what Allah stated in the Holy Quran regarding the endowment of the Holy Land to Qom Mousa (the Jews) in perpetuity.[43] Also, the presence of Jews in the Holy Land, as a sovereign nation, presents a unique theological challenge to many Christian religious leaders. Why? Because almost all Jews reject Jesus as the Messiah and Son of God; and a small number of Jews would like to rebuild the Holy Temple and restore the practice of animal sacrifice, for the atonement of sins,[44] which was banned after the destruction of the Second Temple. In Christianity, Jesus Christ is viewed as the last sacrificial lamb.[45]

10. Might Arabs be getting cheated?

Tenth objection: someone else might say, "But what is in the above deal for the Arabs? It looks as if Arabs are giving up something for nothing." Actually, a lot is in this deal for Arab countries and the Arab people. With this deal, Arab countries would be correcting past errors, amending mistakes, reconciling themselves with God, redeeming their souls, healing their wounds, and liberating themselves from worshipping their Arab identity to worshipping God the Creator of all peoples and all nations, God the Compassionate, the Beneficent, the Merciful.

What could happen if Arab governments were to make such an offer—to grant the Arab Jews the right of return and grant the Arab Palestinians the right of citizenship? Simply put, Arabs would draw themselves closer to the word of Allah.

In the Holy Qur'an, Allah commands the believers to accept peace when offered peace by a foe. But it does not stop there, the following verse says that if the person or entity offering you peace is acting with false pretenses or trickery, then Allah will intervene and bestow his victory on the believers. Here are the verses:

> **"And if they incline to peace, then incline to it and trust in Allah; surely He is the all-Hearing, the all- Knowing. And if the enemy intends to deceive you- then surely Allah is sufficient for you; Allah is the One who strengthened you with His help and with the believers."** (8:61-62)

---

1 - Joshua Teitelbaum, "The Arab Peace Initiative", (Jerusalem: Jerusalem Center for Public Affairs, 2009)
2 - Yaser Burhami, "Jews and Christians are Infidels", El Masry Elyoum, December 25, 2011, pg 3.

3 - Powerful Muslim Arab clerics have a gridlock on the hearts and minds of the majority of the people in the Middle East. This is not a speculative claim. Religious clerics such as Yacoub, Hassan, Burhami or Howaini in Egypt, Hussain of Palestine or Abdul Aziz Al al-Shaikh of KSA who made a recent Fatwa to demolish all non-Muslim places of worship in KSA have tremendous influence on the masses. They can issue assassination fatwas that will be carried out by their adherents, as was the case with the late president Sadat.
4 - Who is this "someone"? The term "someone" is used to refer to certain Muslim clerics, some of whom are described in the above endnote. They do not use a pen to write or a sword to fight, yet they have a much more lethal and loathed weapon—their tongues.
5 - Qur'an 5:82 "Certainly you will find the most violent of people in enmity for those who believe (to be) the Jews and those who are polytheists."
6 - Here at Yale University Common Hall, on November 8, 2012, we had an annual banquet to celebrate the Muslim Festival of Eidul Adha. MSA and the Chaplain's office at Yale chose Provost Salovey to give the key note speech. After the event a Muslim Arab student at Yale came to me in anger: 'MSA made bad choice by having a Jew give the keynote speech' and he invoked Qur'anic text vilifying the Jews; he was then reminded of the Qur'an concept of mercy, he said that mercy only applied to Muslims; and when one attempted to defend MSA for making that choice, one was accused of not being a good Muslim.
7 - Ibid Qur'an 5:33 "The punishment of those who wage war against Allah and His Messenger, and strive with might and main for mischief through the land is: execution, or crucifixion."
8 - Deuteronomy 18:20-22: "But a prophet who presumes to speak in my name anything I have not commanded, or a prophet who speaks in the name of other gods, is to be put to death."
9 - Ibid. Quran 41:34: "Nor can goodness and evil be equal. Repel (Evil) with what is better: Then the person with whom you have enmity will become your friend and intimate!"
10 - Ibid. Quran 41:34: "Nor can goodness and evil be equal. Repel (Evil) with what is better: Then the person with whom you have enmity will become your friend and intimate!"
11 - Ibid. Qur'an 5:8: "O ye who believe! Stand out firmly for Allah, as witnesses to fair dealing, and let not the hatred of others to you (or your hatred of others) cause you to wrong others and to depart from integrity. Have integrity: that is next to piety: and fear Allah, for Allah is well-acquainted with all that you do."
12 - Ibid. Qur'an 45:16: "And certainly We gave the Book and the wisdom and the prophecy to the children of Israel, and We gave them of the goodly things, and We made them excel among the nations."
13 - Ibid. Qur'an 5:60: "Say: Shall I inform you of (him who is) worse than this in retribution from Allah? (Worse is he) whom Allah has cursed and brought His wrath upon, and of whom He made apes and swine, and he who served the Shaitan; these are worse in place and more erring from the straight path."
14 - Q5:43, Q5:44 and Q5:48.
15 - Benzion Netanyahu, The Origins of the Inquisition in Fifteenth Century Spain, (New York: The New York Review of Books, 2001) p65
16 - https://quraish.wordpress.com/2007/08/31/dignitism/
17- https://www.academia.edu/1404941/what_could_happen_if20
18- Ibid. Q60:8.
19 - https://www.academia.edu/3307876/speech_in_Jerusalem
20 - Al Zarkashy, the Pearls of famous Hadith, volume 1, page 167. This Hadith is often cited as "Ulama are the inheritors of Anbi'a (prophets)"

21 - W. N Arafat, "New Light on the Story of Banu Qurayza and the Jews of Medina," *Journal of the Royal Asiatic Society of Great Britain and Ireland*, (1976), pp. 100-107.
22 - Sirat Ibn Hisham, (Cairo: Sirah Publications, 2008) volume 5, p. 20.168 - Al Zarkashy, the Pearls of famous Hadith, volume 1, page 167. This Hadith is often cited as "Ulama are the inheritors of Anbi'a (prophets)"
23 - Ibid., volume 6, p. 26.
24 - John Esposito: What Everyone Needs to Know About Islam (New York: Oxford University Press, 2011) p84.
25 - Norman A. Stillman, The Jews of Arab Land: A History and Source Book (Jewish Publications Society, 1979)
26 - John Esposito: what everyone needs to know about Islam (New York: Oxford University Press, 2011) p88.
27 - Jerusalem Connections Writers Archives, Who is Who in the History of Sephardim.
28 - "Neither the Jews nor the Christians will be satisfied with you [O' Muhammad] unless you follow their doctrine of religion." Quran 2:120.
29 - Abdullah Al Turki, Tafsir Al Tabari, (Ryadh: Dar Aalam al-Kutub, 2003) volume 2, page 484.
30 - Qatada ibn al-Nu'man, quoted in Islamic Research Magazine, General scholarly research and jurisprudence, KSA.
31 - Leviticus 19:34 "The foreigner residing among you must be treated as your native-born. Love them as yourself, for you were foreigners in Egypt. I am the LORD your God."
32 - "Nor can goodness and evil be equal. Repel (Evil) with what is better: Then the person with whom you have enmity will become your friend and intimate!" Qur'an 41:34
33 - Rabbi Patricia Karlin-Neumann, Senior Associate Dean for Religious Life, Stanford University, Letter of Support sent to the International Organization for Peace, March 4, 2009.
34 - Adnan Oktar, "Highlights from Mr. Adnan Oktar's live interview on 12 September 2011", http://harunyahya.com
35 - Background on Israeli POWs and MIAs, The State of Israel Ministry of Foreign Affairs, Retrieved December 4, 2011.
36 - Ivan Watson (July 16, 2008). "Lebanese Celebrate Return of Five Prisoners," Retrieved Dec 14 2011.
37 - Yedioth Ahronoth, Encyclopedia. Retrieved Dec 27 2011.
38 - Richard Spencer, "Israel: Gilad Shalit 'joked with military doctors over health'". *The Daily Telegraph* (London: Telegraph Media Group). Retrieved October 19, 2011.
39 - Sahih Bukhari 1509; Sahih Muslim1333
40 - Lapidoth, Ruth; Ruth E Lapidoth, Moshe Hirsch (1994). The Jerusalem Questionand Its Resolution: Selected Documents. Jerusalem: Martinus Nijhoff. pp. 542.
41 - http://www.jpost.com/Jewish-World/Jewish-News/Chief-Rabbis-reimpose-ban-on-Jews-visiting-Temple-Mount-333741
42 - Ezekiel chapter 40-42.
43 - Q5:21, Q26:59 and 44:28.
44 - Rabbi Joseph Telushkin, Jewish Literacy (New York: Willow Morrow and Company, Inc, 1991), page 60.
45 - John 1:29, 1 Peter 1:19, and Hebrew 10:8

Selected Photographs
FROM THE AUTHOR'S PEACEMAKING ACTIVITIES

Omer Salem, Haram Sharif, Jerusalem
2003

Dahlia, Rehm, Ahmed, Yousef and Sarah enjoy Beitul Hamd in Saila, Fayoum
2004

SELECTED PHOTOGRAPHS

UC Berkeley chancellor and Alumni
2004

On the Haram Sharif in Madinah
2007

Alia, Yousef, Dahlia and Sarah at a Lemon Stand in front of our home in Palo Alto, Califorina
2008

Yousef, Dahlia, Hamid, Sarah, Alia and Omer Palo Alto, California
2008

SELECTED PHOTOGRAPHS

*Omer Salem, Patrick McGaraghan
and Rabbi Lewis.
Palo Alto, Califorina*
2008

*Bernstein, Meir-Levi, Omer Salem, Dr. Mohamed
Abdel Aziz, Dr. Randall Paul, Mr. Ken Allen,
founders of IOP, Palo Alto, Califorina*
2009

Foad Darwish, Daoud Eisa, Omer Salem and Hisham Khairy on the way to the Holy Land
2009

With Druze leaders in Majdal Shams Golan Heights
2009

SELECTED PHOTOGRAPHS

*Sorya, Omer, Professor Fiqui,
Dr. Tamimi and Mr. Eisa, El Saiyyed El Badawi,
Tanta, Egypt*
2012

*Sk. M. Abdallah, Dr. Omer Salem
and Professor Salah el Sawi
AMJA conference, Chicago*
2015

The Grand Imam of al-Azhar and former president of al-Azhar University. Sheikh Ahmed M. el-Taiyyeb, Mashiyyakhet al-Azhar
2010

Omer Salem, Patrick McGaraghan and Rabbi Sheldon Lewis Palo Alto, California
2010

SELECTED PHOTOGRAPHS

Beitul Hamd, Sail-Fayoum where an ME peace treaty is scheduled for April 2020, Inshallah.

Chaplain Omer Bajwa and Muslim Students at Yale University
2012

*Interview on Capitol Hill
with Turkish TV station*
2012

*Rabbi Hollander, Salem, KM Za'iv,
Abrahamson, Dr. Meir, Professor Mordechai,
Knesset, Jerusalem*
2012

SELECTED PHOTOGRAPHS

*Judge Abrahamson, Rabbi Hollander
and Sheikh Tamimi, Hebron, the Holy Land*
2012

*Omer Salem and kids,
Palo Alto, California*
2008

Mr. Faisal, Dr. Salem, Professor Gaafar, Rabbi Abrahamson and Professor Fiqui in Prizren, Kosovo
2014

Dr. Omar Abdel Kafy, Omer Salem and Mohamed Fiqui in South Korea Conference on Religion
2014

SELECTED PHOTOGRAPHS

*Rabbi Hollander, Dr. Gaafar, Dr. Salem, Dr. Fiqui
and Mr. Faisal in Kosovo*
2014

*Professors M. Gaafar and M. Fiqui
and Omer Salem in Kosovo*
2014

Rabbi Nagan, Omer Salem, Hebron
2014

Omer Salem, Rav Mousa ben Saad Dabbagh and Rav Abdullah Mourad, Qaraite sect Jerusalem
2015

SELECTED PHOTOGRAPHS

Al Azhar University Faculty and students at the Mormon Temple in Salt Lake City, Utah
2015

Omer Salem with Gulf Cooperation Council delegation to the UN
2015

THE MISSING PEACE

THE ROLE OF RELIGION IN THE **ARAB-ISRAELI** CONFLICT

section three

Striving for Virtue
DIGNITISM, SCRIPTURE

THE MISSING PEACE

THE ROLE OF RELIGION IN THE **ARAB-ISRAELI** CONFLICT

TOLERANCE
AND RESPECT

The peace promulgated herein is not the peace of one religion dominating over all other religions; Rabbi Jonathan Sacks describes this tyrannical concept ironically, "Our faith speaks of peace; our holy texts praise peace; therefore, if only the world shared our faith and our text there would be peace." [1]

The kind of peace I am proposing here is based on dignitism, a peace based on respecting other people of faith and holding them accountable, through their own imam, rabbi or bishop, to the best their own tradition has to offer.[2] Therefore, a non-Muslim neighbor should read and contemplate a summary of the morals and ethics revealed in the Qur'an, not with the intention of finding faults, fallacies, and contradictions, but with the intention of finding pearls of wisdom and ethical values to understand their Muslim neighbors. By the same token, a Muslim neighbor should read a summary of Biblical ethics, not with the intention of finding faults, contradictions, and controversies but with the intention of finding pearls of wisdom and ethical values to understand their Christian and Jewish neighbors. This way the world will be a much safer and better place to live.

The Muslim's duty is to strive for all virtues according to the Islamic faith tradition and to help others to strive for all virtues according to their own faith traditions. The Muslim who truly understands the teachings of his religion is gentle, friendly and likeable. Honesty and earning trust of one's neighbor is one of the most important duties of a Muslim.[3] Allah created all people and all traditions; and Allah asked the believer to respect Allah's decision to create many nations, peoples, and tongues when He said in the Holy Qur'an, "We have honored only the offspring of Adam." Allah did not say, "We have honored only the faithful offspring of Adam"[4] Allah honored the offspring of Adam without specifying color, creed, religion, or race. Because Allah honored the offspring of Adam, all humans are commanded to do the same.

The only criteria Allah set for such honor is to "strive as" in a race in all virtues."[5] Strive for all virtues, such as forgiveness, humility, prudence, courage, justice, temperance, chastity, charity and patience.

Therefore, if the followers of other traditions are also "striving for all virtues", the best way they know how, and Muslim religious leaders oppose them, then Muslim religious leaders are protesting Allah's plan. The role of Muslims is to "strive as in a race in all virtues" and to help others "strive as in a race in all virtues." [6] This is true Islam as revealed by the Archangel Gabriel to the Prophet Muhammad and his *sahaba* (companions). This is true Islam as believed by the early Muslims who embraced Islam when Islam spread from Arabia, thousands of miles to the east, to India and thousands of miles to the west to Spain, all within less than a century of the death of the Prophet Muhammad. If religious leaders want Allah and Allah's messengers to be pleased with them, they must "strive as in a race in all virtues," and help others to do the same according to their own tradition.

The overarching theme in the Holy Qur'an is, "strive as for a race for all virtues," or "strive for all virtues." The object here is not which of Allah's laws or religions one should follow; rather the object here is to use such law, whether it is in Hebrew, Greek, Latin or Arabic as our basis to "strive for all virtues."

The amazing news about the Holy Qur'an is that it mentions the people of the Book (Jews and Christians) using direct or indirect reference in 4,155 verses out of 6,233 verses in the Holy Quran. That is an astounding 67% of the Holy Qur'an that invites the believer to reflect and ponder on verses that relate directly or indirectly to the people of the Book (Jews and Christians).[7] What could happen if religious leaders exegete the verses in the Qur'an that sum up the meaning discussed here as a basis for Muslims' relationship with Jews and Christians? Allah said in the Holy Qur'an that he created all of us to get to know each other *(lita'arafu)*, to learn to honor and respect each other.[8]

The concept of dignitism discussed earlier is best described by Jonathan Sacks, in his book *The Dignity of Difference: How to Avoid the Clash of Civilizations*. In it, he describes "a way of locating the celebration on diversity at the very heart of the monotheistic imagination." [9]

Dignitism does not mean that anything and everything goes, and it does not mean that religious leaders compromise their own faith to accommodate the way someone else believes. The concept of dignitism is that when a group shows more sincerity and adherence in interpreting and applying the word of God, God will choose that group to lead and rule.

Dignitism does not mean that Muslims and Christians stop proclaiming their gospel.[10] Dignitism encourages both Muslims and Christians to continue to invite others to their faith through their virtuous and righteous deeds, and authentic testimony. Dignitism rejects hypocrisy and relies on sincere persuasion of heart and mind without the least coercion.

God will favor the group that strives the most as in a race for all virtues, and everyone should be joyous for the choice God makes. The idea of "rulership" may be relative to a specific talent or attribute.[11] "Rulership" implies measuring. Thus God could measure us and we could measure ourselves as compared to virtuous people, who "rule" society by virtue and moral values, not by their political position among us. These are the true leaders no matter what job they have in life.

Rulership does not require imposition of power on others by coercion. Allah does not impose Allah's rule over people:

"It is Allah who created you and some are unbelievers, and some that are believers."[12]

Allah leaves it to us humans to select those among us who are fit and qualified to rule.

Prophet Muhammad said in the Hadith tradition "You [people] will be ruled by those who reflect your state."[13] Therefore, if you are in a state of belief *(Iman)* or a state of disbelief *(kufr)* your rulers will reflect such state. There is a political system that God has made perfect for human use that holds moral values that are common to all traditions.[14] However, we can observe from history that any lasting political system has to include a way of changing leadership when the leaders are not acting in the best interest of their constituents. This is how to avoid the tyranny of dictators who use the people's money to pay for a military police to oppress their own people, which is the name of the game in tyrannical regimes. Even if "virtuous" leaders are placed in charge of guns and money, they can easily be turned from virtue, or bequeath power to less virtuous souls. As Lord Edward Acton (d. 1908) said: "power corrupts and absolute power corrupts absolutely," therefore, there have to be checks and balances.

Just as in an Olympic race, the competitor who invests the most time and effort wins the competition. When the winner receives a gold medal, everyone cheers and all are happy for him or her. After all, on the Day of Judgment, all humans will be judged regarding the time they could have been happy and joyful, yet many waste time in conflicts and contempt.

The Italian Rabbi Elijah Benamozegh (d. 1900) developed the concept of "multi-covenantism" which is similar to the concept of dignitism, discussed above. He explains that it is like groups of craftsman who gather to build a great palace for a king. Each group thinks that it is the best and most correct, and it is indeed so, because each group is the best and most perfect in its trade. What one group teaches as the best way for it to build would not be correct for another group. For example a good university cannot operate properly without teachers, administrators and students each excelling at their profession. Mixing of roles between the groups would reduce the specialty and diversity needed to create the most perfect palace. The skills, clothing and training of each group must differ. The goal of all of them is the same, and they should strive as if in a race.

The Purpose of Scripture

What could happen if one takes the Qur'an's word for what it says? What could happen if one did not add one's attitude, disposition or inclinations to the Qur'anic text? This refers to the question: why did Allah send the Prophet Muhammad to the world? The Qur'an tells us that Allah established religions before Islam - Judaism, Christianity, and Noachidism (those who followed Noachidism are referred to as the Sabeans in the Qur'an). Why was a third message introduced?

According to the Qur'an, Allah wanted to restore the religion of the patriarch Abraham (Ibrahim) to the world. So Allah sent the Prophet Muhammad (a descendant of Ibrahim through the line of Ishmael) with a message to restore the religion of Ibrahim. In this case, Allah had to reveal the restoration message in a language other than the previous two languages and to direct the new prophet to worship Allah by facing a new direction. Why? Jews and some Christians prayed facing Jerusalem, just as the early Muslims prayed facing Jerusalem, before Allah commanded the Prophet Muhammad and those who followed him to change their *qibla* (destination) to Mecca in the Hejaz. Then Allah revealed that neither group was to follow the *qibla* of the other group.[15]

So Allah instructed the Prophet Muhammad with a new message in a new language, and proclaimed a new *qibla* that is different from that of Jews and Christians. Why? Because Allah said that Jews and Christians had irreconcilable differences and that the Prophet Muhammad should not get involved, take sides or become entangled in arguments over those differences. The Prophet Muhammad was instructed to stop trying to resolve the dispute between Christians and Jews and to leave that to Allah.[16] In addition, if more than one tradition has the same qibla, it could be a recipe for disaster. If a single site is sacred to two religions, a fight seems inevitable. If what two groups consider to be divine commands are incompatible, they are likely to collide if they share the same space.[17]

Concerning the purpose of the Qur'an for Jews and Christians, there are two main purposes. First, to facilitate reconciliation between Jews and Christians:

> "(O Muhammad) **we have only revealed to you the Holy Qur'an so that you may clarify to them** (Jews and Christians), **those things in which they differ and** (as) **guidance and a mercy for those who believe.**"[18]

With this in mind, Ahlul Qur'an and Ahlul Kitab will enjoy much better relations and avoid much conflict, especially over the Holy Land.

> One might add here that the reason Muslims controlled the Holy Land and dominated the Jews and Christians for many centuries is that they were fighting amongst themselves. Today however, many Jews and Christians agree that the Jews should populate the Holy Land. Muslims should be happy about that and encourage such reconciliation; the Holy Qur'an commands Muslims to reconcile between people.[19]

The second purpose relating to Jews and Christians concerns the unity of basic universal religion. This is revealed in *surah* 44:15

> " . . . **and say (O' Muhammad): I believe in what Allah has revealed of the Book** (Torah and Injil), **and I am commanded to make amends between you; Allah is our Lord and your Lord; we shall have our deeds and you shall have your deeds; There is no contention** (dispute) **between us and you: Allah will gather us together, and to Allah is the return."** [20]

Allah is instructing that there is no contention or dispute "between us and you" because all revelations come from the same source—Allah.

Some might say, but the Qur'an says that the Prophet Muhammad was sent to all mankind, to Arabs and non-Arabs, Jews and

Christians, and all must follow him.[21] To that I say, the Qur'an tells us that every prophet came with a general message and a specific message. The general message is meant for all mankind, this is the *Deen* (universal law) of Islam. In this regard there is no distinction between the prophets.

The specific message refers to the *Shari'a* (covenant) that was assigned to each *Ummah* (nation).

The first religion was given to Adam (pbuh). Jews call this the Noachide covenant since an extra commandment regarding eating meat was added with Noah. Muslims call this first universal covenant Islam. Jews can thus view Judaism as a form of Islam when the term "Islam" is used in its universal sense.

Jews and Christians have their own specific *Shari'a*—their own scriptures and prophets, patriarchs and saints, yet their basic belief systems are consistent with Islam. Thus the Qur'an states that Jews and Christians have a special status within the *Ummah* (nation) of Islam.

The Qur'an is clear about the role of Jews and Christians within the restored religion of the Prophet Ibrahim as revealed to the Prophet Muhammad. As long as Jews and Christians follow the morals and ethics revealed in their own books, they should be left to worship God according to their own conscience, and their assessment will be left to Allah on the Day of Judgment.[22] Just as Allah warns Ahlul Kitab who do not follow the morals and ethics revealed in their scriptures, Allah also has a strong admonition for Ahlul Qur'an who do not follow the morals and ethics revealed in the Holy Qur'an.[23]

The Qur'an was not revealed so that Jews would abandon their faith, their prophet Moses and abrogate their book, the Torah, in order to follow the Prophet Muhammad. The Qur'an was not revealed so that Christians would abandon their faith, their prophet Jesus Christ and abrogate their books—the Greek Septuagint for Protestants or the Latin Vulgate for Catholics—in order to follow the Prophet Muhammad. The Qur'an was revealed for two reasons: Dignitism and d'awa (invitation).[24]

"Dignitism" means to invite Jews to uphold the best morals and ethics that their own tradition has to offer as delineated in the

Hebrew Torah, and to invite Christians to follow and uphold the best morals and ethics their own tradition has to offer as delineated in the Christian Bible.[25]

D'awa means "invitation" or "outreach". It is offered to those Ahlul Kitab who do not follow their faith, or to people who do not have any religion. In one sense, the Prophet Muhammad was sent to invite them all to the restored religion of the Prophet Abraham—Islam. This would mean that Jews, Christians, Noachides and those without any religion are invited to embrace Islam.

However, there is room in Islam to accept Jews, Christians, and Noachides fully as they are, encouraging them to cleave to their faiths and prophets. This holds the view that the *Shari'a* (covenant) of Torah was incorrectly being required of the non-Jewish Edomites, Ammonites and Nabateans of Arabia. At the time of the Prophet Muhammad, Jewish leaders who were keeping a Sadducean-based form of Judaism were competing for power in the Arabian Peninsula and were trying to expand their influence by encouraging converts who were not converted according to the Rabbinic tradition and were not accepted by Rabbinic Jews. Rabbinic Judaism, the continuation of the Pharisaic movement, was at odds with Sadducean Judaism, and it was Sadducean Judaism that was more prevalent in Arabia at the time of Muhammad.[26] The Prophet Muhammad came to release these non-Jews from the *Shari'a* of the Torah, which in the view of Rabbinic Judaism never applied to them, and restore them to the monotheism of the *Shari'a* of the Prophet Abraham (pbuh), otherwise known as Noachidism.[27] Thus, the prophet Muhammed was in that sense in agreement with Rabbinic Judaism vis-a-vis "authentic and inauthentic", and this can serve as a base for conciliation even today.

The Qur'an says that the Prophet Muhammad was sent to offer compassion, grace and mercy to creation and not to coerce, curse or condemn creation.[28] Therefore, if Jews or Christians choose voluntarily to follow the message revealed to the Prophet Muhammad, they are welcome to do so, and they will have their reward doubled, once for following what was revealed to them, and once for following the new message revealed to the Prophet Muhammad, as indicated in the Holy Qur'an.[29]

Jews and Christians should not be taunted, insulted, or ridiculed because they follow a *Shari'a* other than the Prophet Muhammad's Shari'a or a book other than the Holy Qur'an. They should be treated with *Ihsan*—kindness, respect, and integrity. They should be inspired and encouraged to follow the best guidance they have in their own Holy Scriptures.[30] Allah prohibited the believers against reviling, cursing, abusing, or insulting non-Muslim or their deities.[31] Therefore, as Muslims, one should treat others with respect, kindness, and integrity. One should implement the recommendations made in the recent document released from Al Azhar University, Egypt, which promotes "full respect of divine religions . . . . [and to] protect and fully respect [all] places of worship."[32] There should be no coercion, no insults, and no demolition of places of worship. Sadly, there was an Israeli demolition of a mosque in the Negev,[33] and a recent fatwa issued by the Saudi Grand Mufti Sheikh Abdul-Aziz Al al-Shaikh to demolish churches in KSA.[34] It is important for Jews and Muslims to be reminded that God is Merciful,[35] the Prophet Muhammad is a messenger of Mercy,[36] and the Holy Qur'an is the message of Mercy.[37]

We should all be reminded that there is a difference between religion and power politics. Religion is the belief in and worship of a supernatural power called Allah or God. Religion is about relationship with God and kindness to neighbor. Power politics on the other hand is about action by a person or state to increase power or influence over people or states.

Power politics is not concerned with God or with kindness to other human beings. Power politics is about administering resources to maximize state power. Therefore, when a state or a religious leader issues a damaging decree they are in effect practicing power politics, not religion.

The virtue of learning and mercy

What could happen if one thought of Islam as a religion of knowledge, science, and learning? What if one thought that knowledge about revelation and knowledge about creation are the most important values in the Islamic faith?

As to the Qur'an being a book of knowledge and learning, all one has to do is look at the first word revealed to The Prophet Muhammad: "Read!" (Arabic: *Iqra*).[38] God did not start God's revelation by reciting the five pillars of Islam.[39] Allah started the Holy Qur'an by a succinct and powerful command: "Read!" To cement such meaning, the first attribute or quality God chose to describe God's self was not as the creator of heaven and earth as the Book of Genesis has it, not as the creator of the sun and the moon, but as "He who taught with the pen" (Arabic: *Allazi Allama bil qalam*).[40] To affirm these two premises, Allah made a pledge in the Qur'an.

What was the first pledge or vow in the Holy Qur'an? God did not make a vow or a pledge using significant signs like the sun, the moon, the stars, the day or the night, which are all mentioned as pledges later in the Holy Qur'an. The first pledge in the Holy Qur'an is *"Inkwell. We pledge by the pen and by what man writes"*. (Arabic: *Nun. Waal qalam wa-ma yastoroon.*)[41] All of the previous verses were revealed to the Prophet Muhammad to emphasize the virtue of knowledge and learning.

Therefore, the Qur'an is a revelation that emphasizes, in its debut, in its unveiling, in its beginning, the importance of knowledge and learning. When early Muslim scholars and clerics understood such Qur'anic message, the religion of Islam produced many notable and renowned scholars whose work is being studied and taught in Eastern and Western centers of learning. Such scholars include al-Khwārizmī (d. 850 AD) in algebra, al-Razi (d. 925 AD) in medicine, al- Hamadani in physics, al-Farabi in cosmology, al-Kindi (d. 873 AD) in optics, al-Ghazali (d. 1111 AD) in theology, al-Sufi (d. 986 AD) in astronomy, al-Bīrūnī (d. 1048 AD) in physics, Ibn Hayyan (d. 815 AD) in chemistry, Ibn Rushd (d. 1198 AD) in logic, Ibn Khaldun (d. 1406 AD) in economics, and countless other scholars and scientists. [42]

However, the Qur'an draws our attention to an important attribute, quality, and value that precedes learning and knowledge—the foundation on which learning and knowledge (epistemology) firmly rests. That value is *Rahma*, which is usually translated as "mercy, grace or magnanimity." To show that our religion is about mercy and compassion is easy. One could see that in no less than 400 places in the Holy Qur'an the attribute of mercy or compassion is advocated, including in Allah's own name.[43] Also, Allah describes the Prophet Muhammad also as *Rahma*.[44] Therefore, Allah describes Himself as Grace and Mercy, Allah describes the Prophet Muhammad as Grace and Mercy, and Allah describes the Qur'an as Grace and Mercy. To emphasize the importance of mercy and that mercy has to precede knowledge and learning, one reads in the Holy Qur'an that Allah chose that attribute to describe God's self in the first chapter revealed to the Prophet Muhammad.[45]

Also, one reads in the Holy Qur'an that the Israelite prophet Moses spoke to Allah directly and received the Torah from Allah directly. Consequently, the Prophet Moses thought of himself as most learned among his people or the most learned among Allah's creation. Allah wanted to humble the Prophet Moses and to show him that among Allah's vast creation, there exist other servants of Allah who did not receive a holy book from Allah yet are much more knowledgeable than the Prophet Moses. So Allah sent one of Allah's servants to teach Moses that which the Prophet Moses did not know. That servant of Allah was truly the most learned of Allah's creations at the time. Legend has his name as "Khedr" and he possessed a virtue that made him more knowledgeable than the Prophet Moses. That virtue was *Rahma*.[46] This illustrates the Quranic concept that mercy precedes knowledge as a prerequisite for the servant of Allah and as a prerequisite for the follower of the Prophet Muhammad.

Islam acknowledges the prophet Moses and all of those who follow his message as acceptable to Allah. Islam acknowledges Jesus Christ and all of those who follow his message as acceptable to Allah. Each messenger and His followers are good human beings who worship Allah according to the dictates of their own conscience. Therefore, it is possible to be a good human being and worship Allah differently from the way your neighbor worships Allah.

The Holy Qur'an and the Holy Tanakh

Allah admonishes Muslims to apply the knowledge-seeking commandment in the Holy Qur'an.[47] Take a selected group of young Muslim scholars *(ulama)*, about a dozen from each Muslim region, who are versed in Qur'an and in *fiqh* (Islamic jurisprudence), and teach those Muslim scholars biblical Hebrew and the Tanakh. Those Muslim *ulama* will learn the Tanakh, not with the intention of finding faults, flaws, and fallacies, but with the intention of mining those books for pearls of wisdom, cognitive content, accumulated knowledge and proverbs. Those *ulama* could then become the resource for questions about Jews and Judaism.

The goal of having scholars of Arabic and Hebrew reading each other's text in their own tongue has been partially realized. The Talmud was recently translated to Arabic, and the Qur'an and Hadith books are being translated to Hebrew.

It would be worthwhile if governments would support scholars in rendering accurate and faithful representations of the literary heritage of both faith communities.

One of the challenges is that the Tanakh has been translated into more than four hundred and fifty languages, which include many Arabic translations;[48] the Holy Qur'an has been translated into one hundred and five languages, but no official translation to Hebrew.[49] Therefore, one of the most vital roles of the proposed resource ulama mentioned above is to translate the Qur'an into the language of the Tanakh. Why? Many Hebrew scholars, like many Arabic scholars, prefer to read and comment on text published in their own language. By having both the Qur'an in Hebrew, and the Tanakh in Arabic, Arab and Jewish scholars may be able to reach out to each other and help improve relations between both traditions.

Coexistence: The Keys to the Holy Sepulcher

It might surprise you that the keys to one of the most sacred Christian sites, the Christian Church of the Holy Sepulcher, have been entrusted to a Jerusalem Muslim family, the family of Nuseibeh.[50] This family has held the keys to the most sacred Christian site for hundreds of years. Also, Many Jewish families who lived in Jerusalem before 1948 used to leave their children with Arab Muslim families on Yom Kippur and go to the synagogue to worship.[51]

Both the Torah and the Qur'an say that all land belongs to God.[52] God is the true owner of the land. God alone grants permission for possession of the land to certain people for a certain duration. God alone grants the land to whomever God is pleased with. Therefore, the promise for ruling the land is acknowledged in the Qur'an and the conditions by which such ruling can take place is also outlined in the Holy Qur'an. It is appropriate here to emphasize a verse in the Holy Qur'an that seeks common ground in all faith traditions and seeks unity among believers:

> **"And hold fast, all of you together, to the Rope of Allah, and be not divided among yourselves, and remember Allah's favor on you, for you were enemies one to another but Allah joined your hearts together, so that, by Allah's grace, you became brethren; and ye were on the brink of the pit of fire, and Allah saved you from it. Thus Allah makes Allah's signs clear to you, that you may be guided."** [53]

In rabbinic literature it is taught that the strongest rope is a cord made up of three strands. It is my prayer to Allah SWT that the cords of Islam, Christianity and Judaism may be bound together; may religious leaders hold fast to the rope of Allah and not be divided.

Abrahamic Traditions are Helpful Rivals[54]

There is a place under the sun for the Abrahamic religious traditions—Ahlul Qur'an (Muslims) and Ahlul Kitab (Christians and Jews)—to interact respectfully and prosper together. Members of these traditions, inspired by their leading voices, have a clear choice before them. They can either contemptuously avoid interaction or respectfully embrace trustworthy relationships. One choice leads to suspicion, anger and violence; the other to honesty, good will and peace. What message, then, do leaders of these communities need to clearly send?

The answer is simple: They need to tell their people that all members of the Abrahamic traditions were called by God to be righteous rivals—to compete with each other in greater deeds of virtue. They need each other as helpful rivals that prod each other out of complacence in doing good.

For this rivalry to remain healthy, it must be accompanied by the divine virtue of patience. God is patient with the whole world until the final day. Humans need to follow this example. This righteous rivalry can become complicated because some claims of each of the traditions tend to contradict each other in important ways that cannot be denied or compromised. Thus members of each tradition, sincerely and not arrogantly, assert the superiority of their religious doctrines and practices. They believe God wants them to courageously proclaim the truth, and they worry that the critical contest between them over salvatory truth might be superseded by their collaborative contest to surpass each other in worldly good works.

To overcome this concern, the message of rival religious leaders needs to include a call to both *honestly* and *patiently* proclaim their true doctrines. Practically speaking, the honest and patient interaction of rival traditions can produce great religious as well as social benefits. The religious benefit is the test and certification of *faith* and *patience* under the challenge of criticism. This is exquisitely provided when we interact with neighbors that call our faith and patience into question. Thus a Muslim's faith and patience is tried by a neighboring Jew who does not honor Jesus or Mohammed, or by a Christian who worships Jesus and Mary as divine beings. Will the Muslim choose to treat both of them with beautiful perfection *(Ihsan)*? Likewise a modern Christian's faith and patience is not proven until a Christian interacts with critical neighbors: a Jew who rejects Jesus' divinity or a Muslim who calls Jesus and Mary mere human beings. Will the Christian treat both of them with the beautiful perfection of charity? And a modern Jew's faith and patience is not well proved until he or she has Christian neighbors that preach openly that Jesus is the Son of God, or Muslim neighbors who believe that taxing non-Muslims in lieu of military service *(Jizya)* is divinely commanded in Muslim countries.

God has created the world to provide humans the beneficial test of faith and patience. All should be grateful to God for making it such a wonderful and diverse world that includes religious rivals. Each *ummah*, people or nation was given a Prophet, a Book, and a Law. In this very remarkable Muslim scripture God reveals that He could have created us a single people or nation but—for good reason—He chose not to do so:

> "... to each among you have we prescribed a Shariah (law) and Minhaj (custom). If Allah had so willed, He could have made you a single Ummah (people), but (Allah's plan is) to test you in what Allah hath given you: so strive as in a race in all virtues. The goal of you all is to Allah; it is Allah that will show you the truth about the matters in which ye differ." Qur'an 5:48.

---

1 - Jonathan Sacks, The Dignity of Difference (London: Continuum Publishing, 2002) p. 9
2 - "But if they incline to peace, you incline to peace, and trust in Allah. Verily, Allah is the All-Hearer, the All-Knower." Qur'an 8:61
3 - The Prophet Muhammad reported to have said: "Shall I not tell you who among you is most beloved to me and will be closest to me on the Day of Resurrection?" He repeated it two or three times . . . He said, "Those of you who are the best in manners and character." (Ahmad; sahih)
4 - Ibid. Qur'an 17:70
5 - Qur'an 5:48
6 - The Prophet Muhammad (pbuh) said: "My position, in relation to the prophets who came before me, can be explained in the following example: A man erected a building and adorned his edifice with great beauty, but he left an empty niche in the corner [without plaster], where just one brick was missing. People looked around the building and marveled at its beauty, but wondered why a brick was missing from that niche! I am like unto that one missing brick and I am the last in line of the prophets." (Reported by Bukhari and Muslim.)
7 - Ibn Rushd Institute, Independent Research Project, *Ahlul Kitab in the Holy Qur'an.*
8 - "O mankind! We created you from a single (pair) of a male and a female, and made you into nations and tribes, that ye may know "lita'arafu" each other, [not that ye may despise each other]. Verily the most honored of you in the sight of Allah is the person who is the most virtuous of you. And Allah has full knowledge and is well acquainted with all things." Qur'an 49:13. It is interesting that *"lita'arafu"* has the connotation of to acknowledge and recognize, and is related to the root *"bil-ma'rufi"* which means to be fair, honorable, respectable and kind.
9 - Jonathan Sacks, The Dignity of Difference (London: Continuum Publishing, 2002) p. xi.
10 - Judaism is not mentioned here because there is no major and significant missionary movement within Judaism.
11- "Those who believe, those who are Jews, and the Christians and Sabaeans, all who believe in Allah SWT and the Last Day and act rightly, will have their reward with their Lord. They will feel no fear and will know no sorrow." (Surat Al-Baqara 62)
12 - "It is He Who has created you; and of you are some that are Unbelievers, and some that are Believers: and Allah sees well all that ye do." Qur'an 64:2
13 - Daylami in the Book of Ferdous. The contemporary commentator Albany has judged the Hadith as weak. " كما تكونوا يولى عليكم "
14- "So judge between them by what Allah hath revealed" Qur'an 5:48

15 - Ibid. Q2:145. Some Jews and Christians may face Jerusalem when they worship, others may face Shechem, and yet others may face Rome. That is why the Qur'an says that "they will not follow each other's Qibla." And Qur'an 2:145: "Even if you were to bring to the people of the Book [Jews and Christians] all the Signs (together), they would not follow your Qibla (destination); and you are not going to follow their Qibla (destination)."
16 - Ibid. Q6:107: "And if Allah had pleased, they [Jews and Christians] would not have worshipped others [with Allah] and We have not appointed you a keeper over them, and you are not placed in charge of them."
17 - Miroslav Volf, Allah: A Christian Response (New York: HarperCollins Publishers, 2011) pg 5.
18 - Qur'an 16:64
19 - "He who enjoins charity or goodness or reconciliation between people; and does this seeking Allah's pleasure, Allah will give him a mighty reward." Ibid. Q4:114
20 - Ibid. Qur'an 44:15
21 - "We have sent you [O Muhammad] but as a universal (Messenger) to men, giving them glad tidings, and warning them (against sin), but most men understand not." Ibid. Qur'an 34:28
22 - "all of you will return to Allah [on day of Judgment], and Allah will let you know those things you differ about." Ibid. Qur'an 5:48
23 - "for any that disobey Allah and His Messenger - for them is Hell: they shall dwell therein for a long time." Qur'an 72:23
24 - "Dignitism" is a word coined by the author of this book to indicate that people who believe differently from each other still deserve acceptance and respect because we are all created in the image of God. Dignitism implies that there is more than one way to worship God and to be a good human being.
25 - Ibid. Q5:66: "And if they [the Jews] had kept up [the moral and ethical teachings of] the Torah and [the Christians had kept up the moral and ethical teachings of] the Gospel and that which was revealed to them from their Lord, they would certainly have eaten from above them and from beneath their feet (which means to have comfortable and fulfilling lives)"
26 - The **Sadducees** (Hebrew: צְדוּקִים Sĕdûqîm) were a sect of Jews that was active in Judea during the Second Temple period, starting from the second century BCE through the destruction of the Temple in 70 CE. The sect was identified by Josephus (d. 100 AD) with the upper social and economic echelon of Judean society. As a whole, the sect fulfilled various political, social, and religious roles, including maintaining the Temple. The Sadducees are often compared to other contemporaneous sects, including the Pharisees and the Essenes.
The **Pharisees** (/ˈfærəˌsiːz/) were at various times a political party, a social movement, and a school of thought in the Holy Land during the time of Second Temple Judaism. After the destruction of the Second Temple in 70 CE, Pharisaic beliefs became the foundational, liturgical and ritualistic basis for Rabbinic Judaism (the term 'Judaism' today almost always refers to Rabbinic Judaism).
27 - Teshuvot ha-Rambam 2, no. 293
28 - Ibid. Q21:107: "We have only sent thee (O Muhammad) as a Mercy for all humanity."
29 - "They [Jews and Christians] shall be granted their reward twice, because they are steadfast and they repel evil with good and spend out of what We have given them." Ibid. Q28:53
30 - Ibid. Q39:23: "Allah has revealed (from time to time) the most beautiful Message in the form of Books, consistent with itself, (yet) repeating (its teaching in various aspects)."

31 - Ibid. Q6:108: "And insult not those whom they [non-Muslims] worship besides Allah, lest they insult Allah wrongfully without knowledge. Thus we have made alluring to each people their own doings; then to their Lord is their return and [their lord] shall then inform them of all that they used to do."
32 - Associated Press, "Al-Azhar sheik proposes bill of rights, aiming to balance out Islamists in Egypt constitution", The Washington Post Foreign Policy, January 10, 2012
33 - "Israeli police demolish mosque", Algezirah, November 7, 2010.
34 - Bill Getiz, "Persecution on the Peninsula," The Washington Free Beacon, April 6, 2012.
35 - Qur'an 6:54 "your Lord has ordained mercy on Himself,"
36 - Qur'an 21:107 "We sent thee not, but as a Mercy for all creatures."
37 - Qur'an 64:16 "a guide and a mercy to those who believe."
38 - "Read! in the name of thy Lord Who created" Ibid. Q96:1
39 - The five pillars of Islam are: 1) No God but Allah, 2) worship Allah, 3) fast Ramadan, 4) give to charity, and 5) perform Hajj.
40 - This Qur'anic verse is written on the Mascot of Yale University's Sterling Library, one of the oldest universities in the United States. Ibid. Q96:4.
41 - Ibid. Q68:1
42 - Ragheb Al Sergani, "What did Muslims offer to the world?" (Cairo: Iqra for publications, 2009) 253-395
43 - "Allah has inscribed for Himself (the rule of) Rahma" Qur'an 6:54
44 - "And Allah has only sent you (O Muhammad) as a Rahma to all creation." Qur'an 96:3
45 - "Read (Proclaim)! And thy Lord is Most Bountiful (Generous, Merciful)." Qur'an 96:3
46 - "One from among Our servants whom We had granted mercy from Us and whom We had taught knowledge from Ourselves." Qur'an18:65
47 - Nor should the Believers all go forth together: if a contingent from every expedition remained behind, they could devote themselves to studies in religion, and admonish the people when they return to them,- that thus they (may learn) to guard themselves (against evil).Ibid. Qur'an 9:122
48 - Albert C. Sundberg, Jr., "The Septuagint: The Bible of Hellenistic Judaism," The Canon Debate: On the Origins and Formation of the Bible, ed. LM McDonald and JA Sanders (Peabody: Hendrickson Publishers, 2002). pp. 72.
49 - Afnan Fatani, (2006). "Translation and the Qur'an," in Leaman, Oliver. The Qur'an: an encyclopedia. (Great Britain: Routeledge). pp. 657–669.
50 - Michael R. Fischbach, "Nuseibeh Family." In Encyclopedia of the Palestinians, ed. Philip Mattar, New York: Facts on File, 2000.
51 - Yakov M. Rabkin, *A Threat from Within: A Century of Jewish Opposition to Zionism.* (Zed Books/Palgrave Macmillan, 2006) 34.
52 - Qur'an 7:128: "Musa said to the Israelites: Ask help from Allah and be patient; surely the land belong to Allah; He causes such of His servants to inherit the land as He pleases, and the end is for those who guard (against evil)."
53 - (Surat Al Imran 3,103)
54- This chapter was influenced by my colleague at the Foundation of Religious Diplomacy: Dr. Randall Charles Paul, University of Chicago Committee on Social Thought.

THE
MISSING PEACE
THE ROLE OF RELIGION IN THE **ARAB-ISRAELI** CONFLICT

Conclusion

The Middle East is roughly ninety-two percent Muslim and eight percent non-Muslim.[1] Any hope of peace and reconciliation in the Middle East has to come from and be based on the religion of the majority of the people there—Islam. In recent decades, United States and Arab politicians have been trying to find a workable solution—to no avail. From the days of George Marshall in the Truman Administration in the 1950s, to the days of George Shultz in the Reagan Administration in the 1980s to the recent days of George Mitchell in the current Obama Administration, all political solutions have failed. The latest attempt led by George Mitchell failed because, in the words of Tawfik Hamid of the Jerusalem Post, "Solving the Arab-Israeli conflict must be done initially at the theological level rather than the political level, as the former is impeding the latter."[2]

Daniel Levy, a veteran Israeli peace negotiator, said of George Mitchell, "He hit a brick wall."[3] The brick wall of failed politics can be breached if and when religious issues are discussed with openness and sincerity. To effect a lasting peaceful solution to the conflict, two important factors must be considered. The first factor is that the solution must be grounded in the religion of the majority of the people there—Islam. We have already seen that many concepts in Islam are in common with Judaism.

The Imams and scholars listed below are my personal mentors and role models and are united by their deep understanding of the theological message of Islam, their love of God and respect for their fellow. They are also united by their orthodox adherence to Sharia, which acknowledges the multi-covenants that prophet

Muhammad (PBUH) himself recognized in the Hadith and the Holy Quran. They are in turn united by their opposition to all unprovoked and unjustified forms of violence.

We assert that any and all acts of warfare or violence can only occur when ordered by righteous courts or in self-defense, in accordance with Holy Writ. We reject any and all acts of violence executed by individuals acting in an individual capacity. This is especially true when such acts are based upon rumor" or bigotry and directed against unarmed civilians, women, and children as narrated by our Prophet Muhammad.[4]

My mentors today include Professors Dr. Bakr Zaki, Dr. Mohamed Alfiqui and Dr. Yousri Gafaar of Al-Azhar University, Cairo; Dr. Mohamed Q. El-Mansy, of Dar el-Oloom, Cairo; Dr. Abdul Aziz Sachedina of George Mason University; Imam Saad bin Haroun Ilias and Imam Ahmed Lad of the Tablighi Jamaat, New Delhi, India. Also, Imams and Muslim scholars of old who inspire my work include Imam Tahir Ibn Ashour, Imam M. Rashid Reda, Imam Mohamad Abdu, Imam Jalal al-Din al-Suyuti, and Imam Abu Hamed Ghazali.

Religious moral values in the Bible and the Qur'an are the key to a comprehensive and just solution to the Arab-Israeli conflict. Just as Islamic values helped remove corruption in many countries in the Middle East, Islamic values can also be used to peacefully solve the conflict in the Middle East. By emphasizing Islamic moral values, Arab governments will be willing to allow the return of the Oppressed (Arab Palestinians) and the Scattered (Arab Jews) to the lands where they resided, granting dignity to the Arab Palestinians and security to the Arab Jews.

By stressing Islamic moral values, Arabs will focus more on what God emphasized as a priority when God revealed His message to The Prophet Muhammad—namely, knowledge, mercy, and learning. Once Arab governments allow people to worship Allah according to the dictates of their own conscience, then they will find favor in God's eyes. God will then put in the heart of whoever is guarding the Holy Land to allow the Arabs who are followers of the Prophet Muhammad to share in the guarding of the Holy Land, or even be its exclusive guardian. This has happened before in history and could happen again in our lifetime.

It all depends on our vision for the future. It all depends on how religious leaders view our common shared history from a perspective of our common *Deen* (religion), and envision our future as a reconstruction of those times when religious leaders got along.

The Psalter teaches **"O Israel, trust thou in the LORD: He is their help and their shield. O house of Aaron, trust in the LORD: He is their help and their shield. You that fear the LORD, trust in the LORD: He is their help and their shield."** [5] Rabbinic commentary says that Jethro (Prophet Shuayb) was a "B'nai Noah" (righteous non-Jew). The Children of Jethro were referred to as "God fearers" and "Kenites". Targum Onkelos, the official Aramaic translation of the Torah, always translates "Kenites " as Salamai or "Muslamai." In the above verse there are three circles: the Children of Aaron (the priesthood), the Children of Israel, and the God-fearers / Muslamai. In King David's time the Children of Israel, the proto-Muslims and the proto-Christians all worshiped the LORD together.

The book of Acts teaches: God does not show favoritism, but accepts from every nation the one who fears him and does what is right. [6]

In the book of James we read:

> **14 What good is it, my brothers and sisters, if someone claims to have faith but has no deeds? Can such faith save them? 15 Suppose a brother or a sister is without clothes and daily food. 16 If one of you says to them, "Go in peace; keep warm and well fed," but does nothing about their physical needs, what good is it? 17 In the same way, faith by itself, if it is not accompanied by action, is dead. 18 But someone will say, "You have faith; I have deeds." Show me your faith without deeds, and I will show you my faith by my deeds."** [7]

In the Quran we read:

> "Those who believe (in the Qur'an), and those who follow the Jewish (scriptures), and the Christians and the Sabians (followers of Noachide laws),- any who believe in Allah and the Last Day, and work righteousness, shall

have their reward with their Lord; on them shall be no fear, nor shall they grieve." [8]

The Bible and the Quran both call upon people to worship God and to be kind to those who fear God whether they are Jews, Christians or Muslims.

---

1 - Herein the Middle East is defined to consist of the following countries (Egypt, Israel, Iran, Iraq, Jordan, Lebanon, Palestine, KSA, Syria, Turkey) The Future of the Global Muslim Population. Pew Research Center Retrieved 22 December 2011.
2 - Tawfik Hamid, "Why George Mitchell Failed", Jerusalem Post, May 15, 2011.
3 - Daniel Levy, "Mideast Envoy George Mitchell Resigns, 'Hit A Brick Wall' On Israeli-Palestinian Peace Talks", Huff Post World, May 13, 2011
4 - Abu Salih al-Antaki reported that the Messenger of Allah said: "when In a battle, do not kill an elderly or a woman or a child. Do not commit treachery, cut a tree or poison a well." Sunnan Abi Daoud, Hadith number 2613. (Riyadh: Al Rushd Press, 2005), page 1544.
5 - Psalm 115:9 -12
6 - (Acts 10:34-34)
7 - (James 2:14-18)
8 - (Quran 2:62)

Summary Points
TO SOLVE THE CONFLICT

Excerpts from presentation at the Israeli Parliament (Knesset) July 2012, and my Ulama Initiative, Cairo Egypt

This book provides several answers that are compatible with Muslim and Jewish orthodox traditions. Here are several possibilities to improve things, and let's do something new: let's honestly talk together about the pros and cons of these ideas.

The author prefers a one-state solution for Arabs and Jews in the Holy Land. However, in case a two-state solution is the only viable option to peace, and in line with the late King Abdullah Arab Peace Initiative which calls for two-state solution, then one ought to consider the following modified two-state solution:

The international community will finance a railroad connecting Casablanca to Calcutta through Cairo, and connecting Copenhagen to Cape Town through Cairo. Connected to each other, we will get to know our co-religionists with ease.

The following points could serve as basis for a peaceful solution:

- Acknowledge the common heritage and unity by referring to Jews, Christians and Muslims as members of the same Abrahamic religion who worship God with different covenants, languages and customs.
- Confirm the fact that the conflict is part nationalistic and part religious. The conflict is not Islam against the West; it is a complex matter among local peoples who hold ethnic and religious biases. The conflict is not colonial powers against indigenous peoples. It is a local dispute. The conflict is neither secular vs. religious nor inter-religious.

- A religious dispute is easier to resolve through the concept of shared moral values and dignitism. Once the religious dispute is solved, all other aspects of the conflict will be much easier to solve.
- View all people of the region as Ahlul Kitab, people of the book. The Jews have their book, the Christians have their book and the Muslims have their book. One could find harmony among Abrahamic scriptures based on our discussions herein. Scholars from each faith community will study the scriptures of the various *shari'as* in order to further understanding, serving as resources.
- View all people of the region as potential submitters (Muslims) who submit to God under different covenants.
- Emphasize the concept that *Deen* (universal law) is one and Shari'a (covenant) is many. The Jews have their covenant with God, the Christians have their covenant with God, and the Muslims have their covenant with God.

Repartition the Holy Land as follows:

- A Jewish majority state from the Lebanese border in the north to Beersheba in the south and from the Jordan River in the east to the Mediterranean Sea in the west. The state will be called by most Muslims in the world the Northern State of the Holy Land. The state will be majority Jewish. There is precedent for people calling the same place by different names. For example: Egypt is called Misr by Arabs and Egypt by the West.
- The Arabs will have their contiguous state from Gaza and Beersheba in the north to Eilat in the south and from the Jordan international border in the east to the Egyptian border in the west; it will be called the Southern State of the Holy Land. The state will be majority Arab with a minority Jewish population. The state might be called the Southern State of Israel by the Jews around the world. It may be called the Southern State of Palestine by the Arabs.

SUMMARY POINTS TO RESOLVE THE CONFLICT

Which is more
VALUABLE AND IMPORTANT TO ISRAEL?

JERUSALEM

NEGEV

HEBRON

EILAT

- The Southern State of the Holy Land will serve people and traffic moving between the African continent and the Asian continent; that is an important gateway with huge economic, social and political benefits.
- The residents of the Northern State of the Holy Land and the Southern State of the Holy Land will have the right to choose another name for their country by a majority vote of the people, taking into account that the new name does not antagonize the neighbors.
- Defuse the tension caused by the Palestinian refugee problem and the "right of return" by granting all Palestinians citizenship in the countries where they were born or currently reside, and decent housing and social services as all citizens deserve.
- For the small minority of Palestinians who do not wish to be naturalized in their country of birth or residency they would be offered the citizenship of the Northern State of the Holy Land or the Southern State of the Holy Land.
- Unite Jerusalem under the sovereignty of the Northern State of the Holy Land.
- The old city part of Jerusalem will be an International "open city" accessible to visitors from all three faith traditions.

The Arab League to enact the following resolutions

- Acknowledge the new partition plan of historical Palestine.
- Call the two new states created: the Northern State of the Holy Land and the Southern State of the Holy Land, unless they decide to call it something else on their own maps.
- Encourage member states to enact legislations calling for the return of Arab Jews to their communities and their synagogues in the MENA area with full protection for their person and their possessions.

SUMMARY POINTS TO RESOLVE THE CONFLICT

- The newly created Southern State of the Holy Land to be provided with water and electrical energy by Egypt and new housing by KSA.
- Consider all 120 Jewish settlements in the West Bank as legal and part of the Northern State of the Holy Land.
- The Arabs who currently live in the West Bank would become citizens of the Northern State of the Holy Land or move to any Arab country or become citizens of the Southern State of the Holy Land ("SSHL").
- The State of Israel to dismantle the Separation Wall, remove the roadblocks and check points from the West Bank and call itself the Northern State of the Holy Land.
- All commerce and passenger trade handled by the port of Eilat to be redirected through the Suez Canal to the port of Haifa at no extra cost to the Northern State of the Holy Land, or carried by railroad tracks from Eilat to Beersheba.

With the above plan in place, much anticipated peace and prosperity could reign in the Holy Land and beyond. Unites States citizens would be safe traveling in many parts of the Middle East. Muslim jihadi groups would be busy building roads and infrastructures, tying the NSHL and the SSHL to the rest of Asia and Africa.

THE
MISSING PEACE
THE ROLE OF RELIGION IN THE **ARAB-ISRAELI** CONFLICT

Epilogue

The Holy Qur'an calls on all mankind to strive as in a race for all virtues. The call to "strive" is not limited to Muslims and Ahlul Kitab; it is directed towards all humanity. A general universal commandment, it is embedded in our collective consciousness.

Allah created us as nations and tribes so that we can get to know and appreciate each other.[1] Therefore, all of us, all brothers and sisters, living on this spaceship called Earth, are commanded by Allah and rewarded by Allah to "strive". A Muslim, for example, should not be worried or apprehensive about having non-Muslims live next door; on the contrary, one should welcome such an arrangement because this is all part of Allah's plan for the universe.

To build respect and trust without religious compromise is the goal. If we can succeed, our children will enjoy a better world. But even if we do not achieve all our dreams, we will have the honor and reward of having tried. Reconciliation effort is a reward unto itself.

Whether one is Muslim, Jew, Christian, Hindu, Buddhist, Taoist or Confucian, one should be looking to one's own traditions to draw the best morals and ethical values, then strive towards such values and help others to strive towards their own good morals, ethics, virtues, traditions, and values. Allah is generous and just. He sent messengers and prophets to the four corners of the globe to every people, tribe and nation, teaching virtue and ethics in their own tongue. [2]

As we apply the concepts outlined in this book and focus our efforts on peace building measures, we can be confident we are on the right path. Why? We possess the yardstick which determines our relationships with God and neighbor—our respective Holy Scriptures will protect us and all of humanity from going astray.

---

1 - Qur'an 49:13
2 - Qur'an 14:4

THE MISSING PEACE
THE ROLE OF RELIGION IN THE **ARAB-ISRAELI** CONFLICT

Resources

One can never give enough acknowledgements to those who have helped shape one's path over the years. Here is a partial list to those whom I owe gratitude for assisting me in forming my personal vision. The following are scholars, religious leaders, and others whose generous and thoughtful input has greatly influenced my thinking and writing.

Anba Matyros Samir
Ambassador Abdel Aziz Al-Ammar
Ambassador Akiva Tor
Ambassador Elin Solymanov
Ambassador M. Tawfik El Naggar
Ambassador Mahdy Fathalla
Ambassador Nabil El-Orabi
Ambassador Nassir al-Nasser
Ambassador Salah Seleem
Ambassador Ufuk Gokcen
Amnassador Sallama Shakir
Bishop Boyd Smith
Bishop Gordon Scruton
Bishop Richard Jacobsen
Canon Brian Cox
Dr. Abdel Hameed Madqoor
Dr. Abdel Mouty Bayoumi
Dr. Abdul Dayem Nossair
Dr. Abdul-Aziz Sachedina
Dr. Achmat Salie
Dr. Ahmed M. Darwish
Dr. Akram Ghazal
Dr. Ali Shakibai
Dr. Aly el-Samman
Dr. Bakr Zaki Awad
Dr. C. Randall Paul
Dr. Ghada Karmi
Dr. Hala M. Moustafa
Dr. Hamdallah El-Safti
Dr. Hatem (Elhagaly) al-Haj
Dr. Hatem Bazian
Dr. Hatem Zohdy
Dr. Hisham Abdallah
Dr. Hisham Khairy
Dr. Ihsan Bagby
Dr. Ingrid Mattson
Dr. Jonathan Brown
Dr. Kaka Saeed el-Omari
Dr. Karen Armstrong
Dr. Karen Sachs
Dr. M. Abdel Fadeel el-Qusi
Dr. M. Saad Hagras
Dr. M. Salem Abuel Assi
Dr. Magdy Qarqour
Dr. Mohamed A. El-Labban
Dr. Mohamed H. Khalil

Dr. Mustafa Barghouti
Dr. Nady H. El-Attar
Dr. Philip Ackerman-Lieberman
Dr. Philip McCallum
Dr. Salah Alsawy
Dr. Sami Bechir el-Ameri
Dr. Sherif El-Haggan
Dr. Tarek El-Beshri
Dr. Tariq Ramadan
Dr. Wahba El-Tahhan
Dr. Yasser M. Najjar
Dr. Yehezkel Landau
Dr. Yousri Gaafar
Dr. Youssef Ziedan
Father Bishoy William
Father Hanna Kaldouni
Father Salib Girgis
Father Yousef Hanna
General Al-Awady Moustafa
General Khaled Ibrahim
General Medhat Kamal
General Osama Yaseen
Imam Abdul Malik Mujahid
Imam Abdul Moneim Abdullah
Imam Abdullah Antepli
Imam Alaa Bakri
Imam Arif Vohra
Imam Dr. Ahmed M. el-Taiyyeb
Imam Dr. Ekrima Sa'id Sabri
Imam Dr. Jamal Badawi
Imam Dr. M. Qasim El Mansi
Imam Dr. Mohamed al-Fiqui
Imam Dr. Mohamed Hussain
Imam Dr. Mokhtar Maghraoui
Imam Dr. Naeem Baig
Imam Dr. Omar Shahin
Imam Dr. Ragheb El Sergany
Imam Dr. Tahir Kukiqi

Imam Dr. Tayseer al-Tamimi
Imam Dr. Yasir Qadhi
Imam Dr. Yousef Al-Shehabi
Imam Hamza Yusuf
Imam Hassan Nasrallah
Imam Khaled El-Gendy
Imam M. A. H. Qatanani
Imam Mahmoud Al-Saeed
Imam Mohamed Abdel Aziz
Imam Omar bin Suleiman
Imam Omer Bajwa
Imam Salah Nassar
Imam Salman Al-Husaini
Imam Sayed H. Qazwini
Imam Seraj Wahaj
Imam Shamsi Ali
Imam Sohaib Webb
Imam Taha Abdel Sattar
Imam Umer Ilyas
Imam Wathiq Al-Ubaidi
Imam Zaid Shakir
Monsignor Steven Otellini
Mr. A. Hussain Salem
Mr. Abdul Aziz Sakr
Mr. Anthony Mentzer
Mr. Ayman Aniss
Mr. Daniel Piper
Mr. Dauglas Leonard
Mr. David Meir-Levi
Mr. Fouad Darwish
Mr. James Bear
Mr. Jihad Turk
Mr. John Barton, AIA
Mr. John Hanna
Mr. Jonathan Rattner
Mr. K. Khaled Salem
Mr. Kamal El Tahhan
Mr. Karim El-Hibri

RESOURCES

Mr. Kennith Allen
Mr. Lamont Phimester
Mr. Libby Traubman
Mr. Mark Shepherd, Esq.
Mr. Max Mahmoud Shafi
Mr. Mehdi Eliefifi
Mr. Neil Salem
Mr. Othman Nazih
Mr. Patrick McGaraghan
Mr. Raed Salah
Mr. Ralph Bernstein
Mr. Salah Salem
Mr. Sayed Yaseen
Mr. Tad Taube
Mrs. Andrea Schiekel
Mrs. Anne Knight
Mrs. Azza Salem-Ghazal
Mrs. Jenn Waid Paul
Mrs. Jill J. Smith
Mrs. Leah Benstein
Mrs. Len Traubman
Mrs. Rebecca Abrahamson
Mrs. Sheima Salem
Mrs. Vicky Sigworth
Ms. Ann van Brugen
Ms. Enas Kandil-Salem
Ms. Karen Valiasek
Ms. Sarah Fay Salem
Mufti Dr. Ali Gomaa
Mufti Dr. Naim Ternava
Mufti M. Israel el-Nadwi
Mufti Magdy M. Aashour
Pastor John Morehead
Pastor Kenneth Godshall
Prince Ghazi bin Muhammad
Professor Akhterul Wasi
Professor Frank Griffel
Professor Gerhard Böwering

Professor Harold Attridge
Professor M. Ali Hawari
Professor Miroslav Volf
Professor Peter Salovey
Professor Sherman Jackson
Professor Stephen Davis
Rabbi Ari Cartun
Rabbi Benjamin Abrahamson
Rabbi Colin Brodie
Rabbi David Ross Center
Rabbi Douglas Krantz
Rabbi Dr. Burton Visotzky
Rabbi Dr. Reuven Firestone
Rabbi Elie Abadie
Rabbi Ephraim Gabi
Rabbi Herbert Brockman
Rabbi James Ponet
Rabbi Joseph Pesach
Rabbi Lee Weissman
Rabbi Noah Chasses
Rabbi Noah Green
Rabbi Patricia Karlin-Neumann
Rabbi Sheldon Lewis
Rabbi Shmuel Eliyahu
Rabbi Yacov D. Cohen
Rabbi Yacov Nagen
Rabbi Yeshayahu Hollander
Rabbi Yitzchok Feldman
Rabbi Yoel Schwartz
Reverend Dr. Joseph Cumming
Reverend Edward Rawls
Reverend James David Audlin
Reverend Peter Drekmeier
Senator Michael Lee
Senator Richard Blumenthal

THE MISSING PEACE
THE ROLE OF RELIGION IN THE **ARAB-ISRAELI** CONFLICT

Definition of Terms

Arab: A member of a Semitic people inhabiting much of the Middle East and North Africa.

"Arab-ring governments": Egypt, Kingdom of Saudi Arabia ("KSA"), Syria, Lebanon, Jordan, Palestinian Authority and Iraq.

"Arab governments": All twenty-two countries that are members of the Arab League.

Ahlul Kitab: "People of the Book" as defined in the Holy Qur'an, chapter Anaam (6:156). This term usually refers to Jews and Christians. They are people who worship God using the Hebrew *Tanakh* (Bible) and the Greek Gospel.

Ahlul Qur'an: "People of the Qur'an", refers to the followers of Prophet Muhammad - the Muslim people. They are people who worship God using the Arabic Quran.

Bantustan: This term is used to designate areas A and B in the West Bank for the Palestinian people, per the Oslo Accords. They have become apartheid-like ghettos akin to the real Bantustans of apartheid-era South Africa.

Deen: Basic universal law, binding on all humankind. There is one universal deen with many subsets of religious expression or covenants *(sharia)*.

Dhimmi (Arabic): The term used by Muslim conquerors referring to indigenous non-Muslim populations who surrendered by treaty *(dhimma)* to Muslim domination.

Dignitism: The state of living one's religious ideals while honoring those who strive to live their religious ideals. "Religious ideals" means peace with God, self and neighbor. In Arabic we call that *"Ihsan"*. *"Ihsan"* is treating others with respect, integrity and kindness.

Hadith: Sayings of the Prophet Muhammad preserved orally and later written down. (Plural – *ahadith*).

Hasidic Jew: Branch of Judaism that promotes spirituality and joy through the popularization and internalization of Jewish mysticism.

Ihsan (Arabic): "Perfection" or "excellence". Taking one's inner faith *(iman)* and showing it in deeds and actions; a sense of social responsibility borne from religious convictions.

Islam: A monotheistic faith revealed through Prophet Muhammad; the term "Islam" also refers to the monotheistic religions that preceded Muhammad, revealed through Adam, Noah, and Abraham.

Israeli: a native or national of the State of Israel; a person of Israeli descent.

Jihad: To strive, struggle; in Quranic usage, to strive as a servant of God. Connotes struggle against external threats to Islam (lower *Jihad*) as well as one's lower self (higher *Jihad*).

Jizya (Arabic): The money, or tribute, that conquered non-Muslims paid to their Islamic overlords 'with willing submission and while feeling themselves subdued,' to safeguard their existence.

Kabbalah: The ancient Jewish mystical interpretation of the Bible, first transmitted orally, using esoteric methods.

MENA: "Middle East and North Africa", an acronym often used in academic and business writing.

Muslim: A follower of the religion of Islam. In its broader sense, anyone who submits to God.

Muslim Brotherhood: An Islamic religious and political organization, founded in Egypt, dedicated to the establishment of a nation based on Islamic principles.

Orthodox Jew: A Jew who practices strict observance of Mosaic Law. May or may not embrace mysticism.

Palestinian: A member of the native Arab population of the region of Palestine - Israel.

Pious Jew: Similar to orthodox Jew, slightly broader connotations.

Salafi: A Muslim who emphasizes the *Salaf* (predecessors), the earliest Muslims, as model examples of Islamic practice.

Settlers, Israeli: Members of civilian Jewish communities in the West Bank.

Sharia: Covenant; religious practices binding on a specific people. This contrasts with the universal term *"Deen."*

Sufi: A Muslim ascetic and mystic.

Tablighi: Member of *Tablighi Jamaat* (Society for spreading faith), transnational pacifist Muslim movement.

Ummah (Arabic): "Nation" or "community" – some are born into an *Ummah*, but people can join it as well. It is distinguished from *Sha'b* (Arabic) which connotes a nation with common ancestry or geography.

Wahhabi: A member of a strictly orthodox Sunni Muslim sect from Saudi Arabia; strives to purify Islamic beliefs, rejects any innovations.

Zionist: relating to or characteristic of Zionism; "the Zionist movement". A Jewish movement for (originally) the reestablishment and (now) the development and protection of the Jewish nation in Israel.

THE MISSING PEACE

THE ROLE OF RELIGION IN THE **ARAB-ISRAELI** CONFLICT

Exhibits

THE MISSING PEACE

THE ROLE OF RELIGION IN THE **ARAB-ISRAELI** CONFLICT

Exhibit One

FREQUENCY ATTESTING TO
PALESTINE, ISRAEL & JERUSALEM
IN
THE KING JAMES BIBLE

OLD TESTAMENT

	Book name Hebrew	Book name Greek	Book name English	Book name Arabic	Number of chapters	Number of verses
1.	בראשית	Γένεσις Génesis	Genesis	التكوين	50	1533
2.	שמות	Ἔξοδος Éxodos	Exodus	الخروج	40	1213
3.	ויקרא	Λευϊτικόν Leuitikón	Leviticus	اللاويين	27	859
4.	במדבר	Ἀριθμοί Arithmoí	Numbers	العدد	36	1288
5.	דברים	Δευτερονόμιον Deuteronómion	Deuteronomy	التثنية	34	959
6.	יהושע	Ἰησοῦς Ναυῆ Iêsous Nauê	Joshua	يشوع	24	658
7.	שופטים	Κριταί Kritaí	Judges	القضاة	21	618
8.	רות	Ῥούθ Roúth	Ruth	راعوث	4	85
9.	(שמואל א)	Βασιλειῶν Αʹ 1 Reigns	1 Samuel	صموئيل الأول	31	810

143

10.	שמואל (ב)	Βασιλειῶν Β' II Reigns	2 Samuel	صموائيل الثاني	24	695
11.	מלכים (א)	Βασιλειῶν Γ' III Reigns	1 Kings	الملوك الأول	22	816
12.	מלכים (ב)	Βασιλειῶν Δ' IV Reigns	2 Kings	الملوك الثاني	25	719
13.	דברי הימים (א)	Παραλειπομένων Α' I Paralipomenon	1 Chronicles	أخبار الأيام الأول	29	942
14.	דברי הימים (ב)	Παραλειπομένων Β' II Paralipomenon	2 Chronicles	أخبار الأيام الثاني	36	822
15.	עזרא	Ἔσδρας Α' I Esdras	Ezra	عزرا	10	280
16.	נחמיה	Ἔσδρας Β' II Esdras	Nehemiah	نحمايا	13	406
17.	אסתר	Ἐσθήρ Esther	Esther	أستير	10	167
18.	איוב	Ἰώβ Iōb	Job	أيوب	42	270
19.	תהילים	Ψαλμοί psalmoi	Psalm	المزامير	150	2461
20.	משלי	Παροιμίαι Paroimiai	Proverbs	الأمثال	31	915
21.	קהלת	Ἐκκλησιαστής Ἐκκλησιαστής	Ecclesiastes	الجامعة	12	222
22.	שיר השירים	Ἄσμα Ἀσμάτων Asma Asmaton	Song of Solomon	نشيد الإنشاد	8	117

EXHIBITS

23.	ישעיה	Ἡσαΐας Hesaias	Isaiah	إشعياء	66	1292
24.	ירמיה	Ἰερεμίας Hieremias	Jeremiah	إرميا	52	1364
25.	איכה	Θρῆνοι Ἰερεμίου Thrênoi Ieremíou	Lamentations	مراثي إرميا	5	154
26.	יחזקאל	Ἰεζεκιήλ Iezekiêl	Ezekiel	حزقيال	48	1273
27.	דניאל	Δανιήλ Daniêl	Daniel	دانيال	12	357
28.	הושע	Ὡσηέ Α' I. Osëe	Hosea	هوشع	14	197
29.	יואל	Ἰωήλ Δ' IV. Ioël	Joel	يوئيل	3	73
30.	עמוס	Ἀμώς Β' II. Amōs	Amos	عاموس	9	146
31.	עבדיה	Ὀβδίου Ε' V. Obdias	Obadiah	عوبديا	1	21
32.	יונה	Ἰωνᾶς Ϛ' VI. Ionas	Jonah	يونان	4	48
33.	מיכה	Μιχαίας Γ' III. Michaias	Micah	ميخا	7	105
34.	נחום	Ναούμ Ζ' VII. Naoum	Nahum	ناحوم	3	47
35.	חבקוק	VIII. Ambakum Ἀμβακούμ Η'	Habakkuk	حبقوق	3	56
36.	צפניה	Σοφονίας Θ' IX. Sophonias	Zephaniah	صافنيا	3	53

37.	חגי	Ἀγγαῖος Ι' X. Angaios	Haggai	حجي	2	38
38.	זכריה	Ζαχαρίας ΙΑ ΧΙ. Zacharias	Zechariah	زكريا	14	211
39.	מלאכי	Ἄγγελος ΙΒ' XII. Messenger	Malachi	ملاخي	4	55
				Total (OT)	929	23145

NEW TESTAMENT

40		ΚΑΤΑ ΜΑΤΘΑΙΟΝ	Matthew	إنجيل متى	28	1071
41		ΚΑΤΑ ΜΑΡΚΟΝ	Mark	إنجيل مرقس	16	678
42		ΚΑΤΑ ΛΟΥΚΑΝ	Luke	إنجيل لوقا	24	1151
43		ΚΑΤΑ ΙΩΑΝΝΗΝ	John	إنجيل يوحنا	21	879
44		ΠΡΑΞΕΙΣ ΤΩΝ ΑΠΟΣΤΟΛΩΝ	Acts	أعمال الرسل	28	1007
45		ΠΡΟΣ ΡΩΜΑΙΟΥΣ	Romans	الرومانيين	16	433
46		ΠΡΟΣ ΚΟΡΙΝΘΙΟΥΣ Α'	1 Corinthians	الأولى إلى الكورنثيين	16	437
47		ΠΡΟΣ ΚΟΡΙΝΘΙΟΥΣ Β'	2 Corinthians	الثانية إلى الكورنثيين	13	257
48		ΠΡΟΣ ΓΑΛΑΤΑΣ	Galatians	الغلاطيين	6	149

EXHIBITS

49	ΠΡΟΣ ΕΦΕΣΙΟΥΣ	Ephesians	الإفسسيين	6	155
50	ΠΡΟΣ ΦΙΛΙΠΠΗΣΙΟΥΣ	Philippians	الفيلبيين	4	104
51	ΠΡΟΣ ΚΟΛΟΣΣΑΕΙΣ	Colossians	كولوسي	4	95
52	ΠΡΟΣ ΘΕΣΣΑΛΟΝΙΚΕΙΣ Α	1 Thessalonians	الأولى إلى التسالونيكيين	5	89
53	ΠΡΟΣ ΘΕΣΣΑΛΟΝΙΚΕΙΣ Β΄	2 Thessalonians	الثانية إلى التسالونيكيين	3	47
54	ΠΡΟΣ ΤΙΜΟΘΕΟΝ Α΄	1 Timothy	الأولى إلى تيموثاوس	6	113
55	ΠΡΟΣ ΤΙΜΟΘΕΟΝ Β΄	2 Timothy	الثانية إلى تيموثاوس	4	83
56	ΠΡΟΣ ΤΙΤΟΝ	Titus	تيطس	4	46
57	ΠΡΟΣ ΦΙΛΗΜΟΝΑ	Philemon	فيلمون	1	25
58	ΠΡΟΣ ΕΒΡΑΙΟΥΣ	Hebrews	العبرانيين	13	303
59	ΙΑΚΩΒΟΥ	James	رسالة يعقوب	5	108
60	ΠΕΤΡΟΥ Α΄	1 Peter	رسالة بطرس الأولى	5	105
61	ΠΕΤΡΟΥ Β΄	2 Peter	رسالة بطرس الثانية	3	61
62	ΙΩΑΝΝΟΥ Α΄	1 John	رسالة يوحنا الأولى	5	105

63		ΙΩΑΝΝΟΥ Β΄	2 John	رسالة يوحنا الثانية	1	13
64		ΙΩΑΝΝΟΥ Γ΄	3 John	رسالة يوحنا الثالثة	1	15
65		ΙΟΥΔΑ	Jude	رسالة يهوذا	1	25
66		ΑΠΟΚΑΛΥΨΙΣ ΙΩΑΝΝΟΥ	Revelation	سفر الرؤيا	22	404
				Total (NT)	260	7958
				Total	1189	31173

EXHIBIT TWO

FREQUENCY ATTESTING TO PALESTINE, ISRAEL & AHLUL KITAB THE HOLY QUR'AN

Sura Number	Anglicized name	اسم السورة	English Translation	Frequency of Ahlul Kitab[1]
1	al-Fatihah	الفاتحة	The Opening	2
2	al-Baqarah	البقرة	The Cow	185
3	Al-Imran	آل عمران	The Family Of Imran	140
4	an-Nisa'	النساء	Women	56
5	al-Ma'idah	المائدة	The Food	84
6	al-An`am	الانعام	The Cattle	72
7	al-A`raf	الاعراف	The Elevated Places	175
8	al-Anfal	الانفال	The Spoils Of War	3
9	at-Taubah	التبة	Repentance	39
10	Yunus	يونس	Jonah	33
11	Hud	هود	Hud	77
12	Yusuf	يوسف	Joseph	101
13	ar-Ra`d	الرعد	The Thunder	12
14	Ibrahim	ابراهيم	Abraham	22
15	al-Hijr	الحجر	The Rock	39
16	an-Nahl	النحل	The Bee	33
17	bani Isra'il	بني اسرائيل	The Israelites	36
18	al-Kahf	الكهف	The Cave	65
19	Maryam	مريم	Mary	75
20	Ta Ha	طه (موسى)	Ta Ha	110
21	al-Anbiya'	الانبياء	The Prophets	70
22	al-Hajj	الحج	The Pilgrimage	22
23	al-Mu'minun	المؤمنون	The Believers	21
24	an-Nur	النور	The Light	2
25	al-Furqan	الفرقان	The Criterion	8
26	ash-Shu`ara'	الشعراء	The Poets	160
27	an-Naml	النمل (سليمان)	The Ant	55
28	al-Qasas	القصص	The Narrative	66
29	al-`Ankabut	العنكبوت	The Spider	23
30	ar-Rum	الروم	The Romans	4
31	Luqman	لقمان	Lukman	2

---

[1] Ahlul Kitab is a term that includes Jews, Christians and Israelites.

32	as-Sajdah	السجدة	The Adoration	8
33	al-Ahzab	الاحزاب	The Allies	5
34	Saba'	سبأ	Sheba	6
35	al-Fatir	الفاطر	The Creator	15
36	Ya Sin	ياسين	Ya Sin	20
37	as-Saffat	الصافات	The Rangers	82
38	Sad	ص (داوود)	Sad	33
39	az-Zumar	الزمر	The Companies	4
40	al-Mu'min	المؤمن	The Forgiving One	39
41	Fussillat	فصلت	Revelations Well	2
42	ash-Shura	الشورى	The Counsel	8
43	az-Zukhruf	الزخرف	The Embellishment	2
44	ad-Dukhan	الدخان	The Evident Smoke	17
45	al-Jathiyah	الجاثية	The Kneeling	4
46	al-Ahqaf	الاحقاف	The Sandhills	4
47	Muhammad	محمد	Muhammad	2
48	al-Fath	الفتح	The Victory	2
49	al-Hujurat	الحجرات	The Chambers	0
50	Qaf	قاف	Qaf	4
51	adh-Dhariyat	الذاريات	The Scatterers	23
52	at-Tur	التور	The Mountain	1
53	an-Najm	النجم	The Star	18
54	al-Qamar	القمر	The Moon	27
55	ar-Rahman	الرحمن	The Merciful	0
56	al-Waqi`ah	الواقعة	That Which is Coming	0
57	al-Hadid	الحديد	The Iron	4
58	al-Mujadilah	المجادلة	She Who Pleaded	0
59	al-Hashr	الحشر	The Exile	8
60	al-Mumtahanah	الممتحنة	She Who is Tested	6
61	as-Saff	الصف	The Ranks	3
62	al-Jumu`ah	الجمعة	The Day of Congregation	4
63	al-Munafiqun	المنافقون	The Hypocrites	1
64	at-Taghabun	التغابن	The Cheating	0
65	at-Talaq,	الطلاق	The Divorce	0
66	at-Tahrim	التحريم	The Prohibition	3
67	al-Mulk	الملك	The Kingdom	0
68	al-Qalam	القلم	The Pen	20
69	al-Haqqah	الحاقة	The Inevitable	3
70	al-Ma`arij	المعارج	The Ladders	0
71	Nuh	نوح	Noah	28
72	al-Jinn	الجن	The Jinn	0
73	al-Muzammil	المزمل	The Mantled One	2
74	al-Mudathir	المدثر	The Clothed One	0

EXHIBITS

#	Name	Arabic	English	
75	al-Qiyamah	القيامة	The Resurrection	0
76	al-Insane	الانسان	The Man	0
77	al-Mursalat	المرسلات	The Emissaries	0
78	an-Naba'	النباء	The Tidings	0
79	an-Nazi`at	النازعات	Those Who Pull Out	12
80	`Abasa	عبس	He Frowned	0
81	at-Takwir	التكوير	The Cessation	0
82	al-Infitar	الانفطار	The Cleaving Asunder	0
83	at-Mutafifeen	المطففين	The Defrauders	0
84	al-Inshiqaq	الانشقاق	The Rending	0
85	al-Buruj	البروج	the Constellations	11
86	at-Tariq	الطارق	The Night-Comer	0
87	al-A`la	الأعلى	The Most High	2
88	al-Ghashiya	الغاشية	The Overwhelming Calamity	0
89	al-Fajr	الفجر	The Dawn	0
90	al-Balad	البلد	The City	0
91	ash-Shams	الشمس	The Sun	0
92	al-Layl	الليل	The Night	0
93	ad-Duha	الضحى	The Early Hours	0
94	al-Inshirah	الانشراح	The Expansion	0
95	at-Tin	التين	The Fig	0
96	al-`Alaq	العلق	The Clot	0
97	al-qadr	القدر	The Majesty	0
98	al-Bayyinah	البينة	The Proof	5
99	al-Zilzal	الزلزلة	The Shaking	0
100	al-`Adiyat	العاديات	The Assaulters	0
101	al-Qari`ah	القارعة	The Terrible Calamity	0
102	at-Takathur	التكاثر	Worldly Gain	0
103	al-`Asr	العصر	Time	0
104	al-Humazah	الهمزة	The Slanderer	0
105	al-Fil	الفيل	The Elephant	0
106	Quraysh	قريش	The Quraish	0
107	al-Ma`un	الماعون	The Daily Necessaries	0
108	al-Kauthar	الكوثر	Abundance	0
109	al-Kafirun	الكافرون	The Unbelievers	0
110	an-Nasr	النصر	The Help	0
111	al-Lahab	ابو لهب	The Flame	0
112	al-Ikhlas	الاخلاص	The Unity	0
113	al-Falaq	الفلق	The Daybreak	0
114	an-Nas	الناس	The Men	0

151

EXHIBIT THREE

Ethnic Cleansing of Jews from the Arab World

"WHEN I SEE A JEW BEFORE ME, I KILL HIM. IF EVERY ARAB DID THIS, IT WOULD BE THE END OF THE JEWS."
— Syrian Minister of Defense Mustafa Tlass

	# of Jews in 1948	Today
Algeria	140,000	100
Egypt	75,000	100
Iraq	150,000	35
Lebanon	20,000	100
Libya	38,000	0
Morocco	265,000	5,500
Syria	30,000	100
Tunisia	105,000	1,500
Yemen	55,000	200

AN ENTIRE HISTORY ERASED
Arab Jews lived as 2nd class citizens in the Arab world for centuries until the mid 20th century, when systematic policies of ethnic cleansing began.

MASS MURDER
Massacres were carried out against Jewish communities, which had existed for centuries. Arab governments removed Jewish communities in order to push them out of the country.

STRIPPED OF CITIZENSHIP
Jews in countries such as Libya and Syria were stripped of their citizenship for no reason, only because they were Jews. They became stateless refugees, and were forced to find a new home.

CONFISCATION OF PROPERTY
Arab governments seized homes, businesses, bank accounts, and property. When expelled, Jews were only allowed to leave with one suitcase and little or no cash. Arab Jews told everything they had.

SYNAGOGUES DESTROYED
As a final step, Jewish places of worship were destroyed, leaving little evidence of what was once known as Arab Jewry. Today, most Arab Jews live in Israel and the United States of America.

Number of Jews in the Arab World: 878,000 (1948) → 7,635 (Today)

... and now they say the Jewish State does not have a right to exist ...

When will this hatred end?

Exhibit Four
POSSIBLE LAND SWAP BETWEEN ISRAEL AND PALESTINE

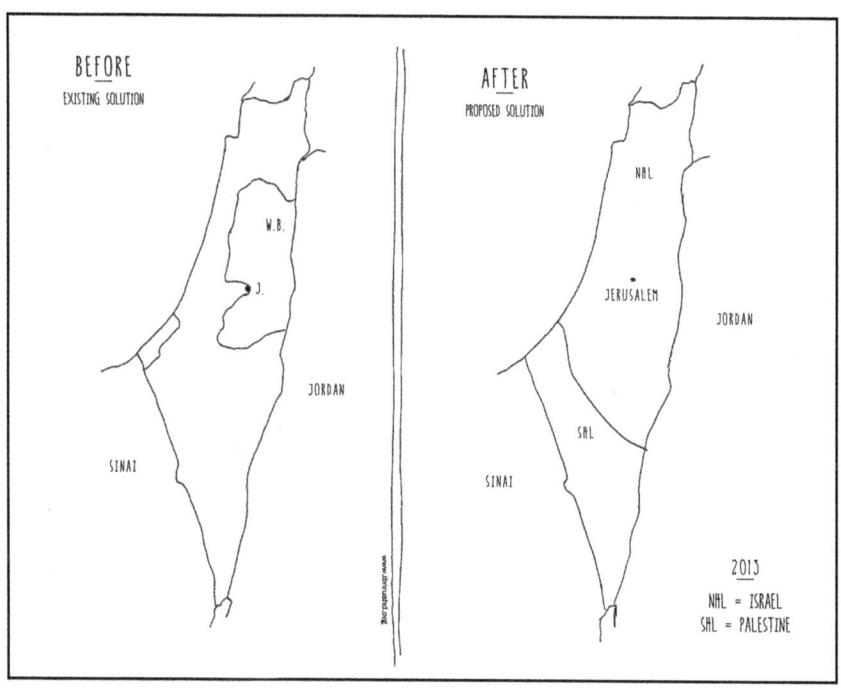

Exhibit Five
POSSIBLE LAND SWAP BETWEEN EGYPT, ISRAEL AND PALESTINE

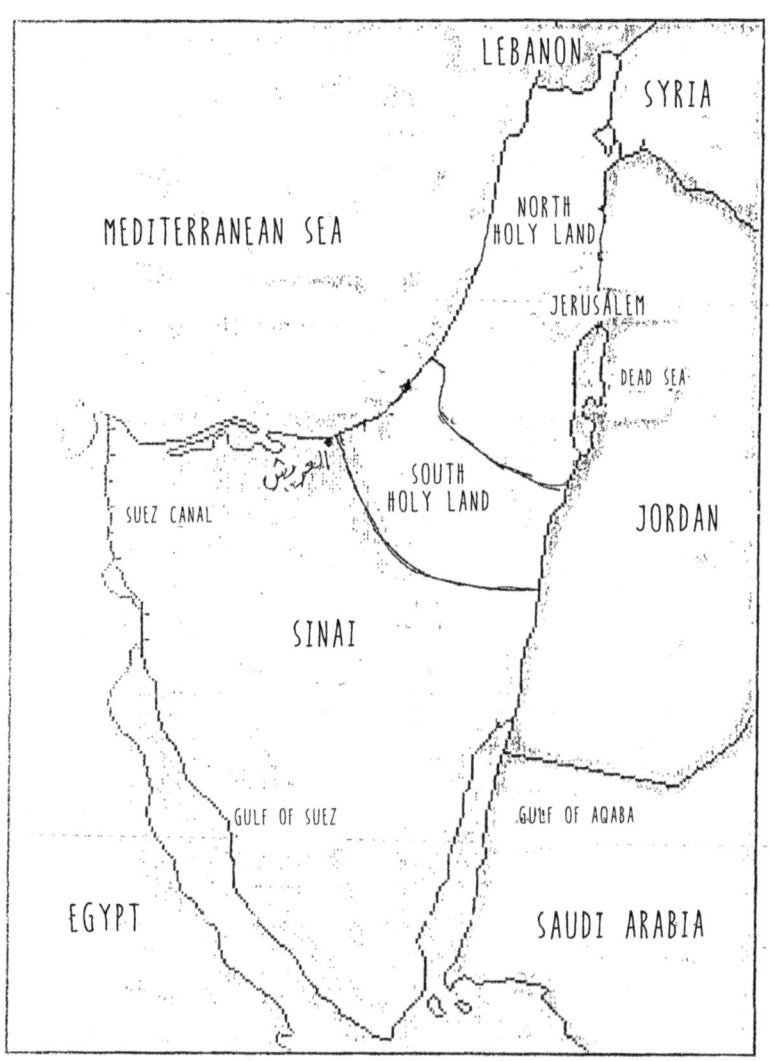

Exhibit Six
MAP OF THE TWELVE TRIBES OF ISRAEL

THE
MISSING PEACE
THE ROLE OF RELIGION IN THE **ARAB-ISRAELI** CONFLICT

BIBLIOGRAPHY

1. Rachel Scott, *The Challenge of Political Islam* , (Stanford: Stanford University Press, 2010).
2. Carl Brown, *Religion and State*, (New York: Columbia University Press, 2000)
3. John Esposito, *Makers of Contemporary Islam*, (Oxford: Oxford University Press, 2001)
4. Shireen Hunter, *Modernization, Democracy and Islam*, (Westport: Preager Publishers, 2005)
5. S. Ayse Kadayifci-Orellana, *Standing on an Isthmus*, (Plymouth: Lexington Books, 2007)
6. Ellen Lust, *The Middle East*, (Stanford: CQ Press, 2010)
7. John Esposito, *What Everyone Needs to know about Islam,* (Oxford: Oxford University Press, 2001)
8. W. Montgomery Watt, *Islamic Philosophy and Theology* , (New Jersy: Aldine Publishers, 2009)
9. Mark R. Cohen, *Under Crescent and Cross*, (Princeton: Princeton University Press, 1996)
10. Kenneth Craig, *Muhammad and the Christian*, (Oxford: One world Publication, 1999)
11. Bernard Lewis, *What Went Wrong?* , (New York: Oxford University Press, 2002)
12. Kenneth Craig, *The Call of the Minaret,* (New York: Oxford University Press, 1964)

13. Jacob Lassner, *Jews and Muslims in the Arab World,* (Maryland: Rowman and Littlefield publishers, 2007)
14. Michael Laskier and Yacoob Lev, *The Convergence of Judaism and Islam,* (Gainsville: University Press of Florida, 2011)
15. Jonathan Sacks, *The Dignity of Difference*, (London: Continuum Press, 2002)
16. Raymond Baker, *Islam Without Fear,* (Boston: Harvard Collage Press, 2003)
17. Norman Stillman, *The Jews of Arab Lands,* (Oxford: Oxford University Press, 1979)
18. David Liepert, *Muslim Christian and Jew*, (Toronto: Faith and Life Publishing, 2010)
19. Miroslav Volf, *A Public Faith*, (Grand Rapids: Brazos Press, 2011)
20. Rachel Scot, *The Challenge of Political Islam*, (Stanford: Stanford University Press, 2010)
21. Miroslav Volf, *Allah: A Christian Response,* (New York: Harper Collins Publishers, 2011)
22. Peter L. Burger, *"The Desecularization of the World"*, (Michigan: Wm. B. Eerdmans Publishing, 1999)
23. Abdullah Yûsuf Ali, *The Meaning of the Holy Qur'an,* (Maryland: Amana Publications, 2009)
24. Malka H. Schlewitz, *The Forgotten Millions: the Modern Jewish Exodus from Arab Land* (New York: Continuum, 2000).
25. James Carroll, *Constantine's Sword: The Church and the Jews* (New York, Houghton Mifflin Company, 2001)

Arabic

LETTERS OF SUPPORT

د/ سعيد الأعظمي الندوي
رئيس تحرير :
مجلة البعث الإسلامي

Dr. Saeed Al Azami Al Nadwi
Chief Editor :
"Albaas el Islami"

T5-49-2011

تزكية لتنفيذ فكرة معهد ابن رشد في الولايات المتحدة

الحمد لله رب العالمين، والصلاة والسلام على إمام المرسلين والمتقين محمد بن عبد الله الأمين عليه وعلى آله وصحبه ومن اهتدى بهديه صلوات الله وسلامه عليهم بصفة دائمة مستمرة إلى يوم الدين.

هناك فكرة إنشاء معهد ابن رشد لإيجاد الحوار المتمدن بأسلوب أصيل معاصر بين الديانات ودين الإسلام، وقد تولى هذه الفكرة الإيجابية البناءة فضيلة الأخ الأكرم **عمر أحمد سالم** من الجمهورية المصرية والمقيم حاليا في كاليفورنيا بالولايات المتحدة كداعية، مبعوث من مصر إلى أمريكا، وسوف يهدف هذا المعهد إلى تفعيل قيم التسامح والتفاهم بين المجتمعات والشعوب وتوجيهها إلى تركيز الجهود على التعاون من كل نوع، حتى يصلح المجتمع ويسعد البشر، ويسود المنهج الإسلامي في جميع المجتمعات والبيئات وعلى جميع المستويات.

إنني أبارك هذه الفكرة الجميلة وابتهل إلى الله تعالى أن يمهد الطريق لتحقيقها في أقرب وقت إن شاء الله تعالى، ويكتب لسعادة الدكتور عمر أحمد سالم التوفيق الكامل لإنشاء هذا المعهد الرشيد ويوفر له من الوسائل ما لا يحتاج بعده إلى شيئ آخر.

والله هو الموفق للصواب.

كتبه بيمينه

سعيد الأعظمي الندوي
رئيس تحرير مجلة البعث الإسلامي
ندوة العلماء لكهنؤ الهند

١٤٣٢/٠٣/١٥ هـ
٢٠١١/٠٢/١٩ م

ARABIC LETTERS OF SUPPORT

Dr. Mufti Zahid A. Khan
Director,
Religious Affairs, Aligarh Muslim University
Aligarh-202002 (INDIA)
Ph: 91-571-2700049 (O), 2708786 (R)
M: 09359940609, Fax. 91-571-2702607, 2701166
E-mail: muftizahid@yahoo.com

د/ مفتى زاهد على خان
مدير الشؤون الدينية
الجامعة الإسلامية، على كره (الهند)

Ref. No .... الرقم .... Dated .... التاريخ ....

بسم الله الرحمن الرحيم

تزكية لتنفيذ فكرة معهد ابن رشد فى جمهورية مصر العربية وفى الولايات المتحدة الأمريكية

الحمد لله رب العالمين والسلام على الأنبياء والمرسلين والصلوة على خاتم النبيين وعلى آله وصحبه أجمعين ومن تبعهم بإحسان إلى يوم الدين، أما بعد

هناك فكرة إنشاء معهد ابن رشد لإيجاد الحوار المتمدن بأسلوب صحيح معاصر بين الديانات ودين الإسلام، وقد أجاد هذه الفكرة الإيجابية القويمة مطابقاً بسنة السلف الصالح فضيلة الأستاذ عمر بن احمد بن عباس سالم رئيس معها. ابن رشد للحوار المتمدن من جمهورية مصر العربية والمقيم حاليا فى كاليفورنيا بالولايات المتحدة الأمريكية، مبعوث من مصر إلى امريكا، وسوف يهدف هذا المعهد الى تفعيل قيم التسامح والتفاهم بين المجتمعات والشعوب، ويسود المنهج الاسلامى فى جميع المجتمعات والبيئات وعلى جميع المستويات، وللحوار المتمدن يجب ترك التطرف والعنف والإرهاب من أصحاب الديانات كلها ودين الإسلام.

إنى أبارك هذه الفكرة الجميلة وابتهل إلى الله أن يمهد الطريق إلى الصواب ويكتب بسعادة الدكتور عمر بن أحمد بن عباس سالم التوفيق لإنشاء هذا المعهد الرشيد و أن يوفر له من الوسائل كلها.

كتبه بأعماق قلبه

(د/ مفتى زاهد على خان)
مدير الشؤون الدينية
الجامعة الإسلامية على كره (الهند)

١٤٣٢/٣/١٩ هـ
٢٠١١/٢/٢٣ م

Res: "Mary's Garden" -(B-08), Zakaullah Road, Tar Bungalow, AMU, Aligarh 202002 (INDIA)

الرقم: .... التاريخ: ٢٠١١/٣/٢٤م

بسم الله الرحمن الرحيم

الحمد لله رب العالمين نحمده ونصلي على رسوله الأمين وعلى آله وصحبه أجمعين.

علمنا من فضيلة الشيخ/ عمر أحمد سالم أنه بصدد انشاء معهد يسمى "معهد ابن رشد للحوار" بفرعيها بجمهورية مصر العربية والولايات المتحدة الأمريكية. ومن أهم أهداف هذا المعهد تفعيل قيم التسامح والتفاهم بين مجتمعات العالم والتعاون الاقتصادي والثقافي والتنموي بين الشعوب ومواجهة الأفكار المتطرفة وإعداد مقررات ومناهج دراسية تدعو إلى الحوار ونبذ العنف.

اننا إذ نبارك فضيلة الشيخ/ عمر أحمد سالم في جهوده وخدماته ندعو له بالتوفيق والسداد ونرجو من الجميع التعاون. والله من وراء القصد وهو ولي التوفيق.

أ. علي باوتي

مدير الجامعة الإسلامية بكيرالا

ARABIC LETTERS OF SUPPORT

بسم الله الرحمن الرحيم

جامعة دار السلام
عمرآباد ٦٣٥ ٨٠٨ ـ الهند

كاكا سعيد أحمد العمري
الأمين العام

الرقم : 2011/573/17
التاريخ : 1432/04/28 هـ
الموافق : 2011/04/03 م

فضيلة الشيخ / عمر سالم المحترم حفظه الله ورعاه .
السلام عليكم ورحمة الله وبركاته تحية طيبة مباركة ،
نرجو لكم دوام الخير والعافية ،

تهدي "إدارة جامعة دارالسلام عمرآباد" مع تحية الإسلام المباركة بتقدم أسمى آيات الإحترام والشكر على زيارتكم خلال جولاتكم العلمية والتوجيهية في منطقة جنوب الهند وتخص بالذكر مدى أهمية كلمتكم في رحاب مسجدنا أمام أعضاء التدريس وفئة الطلبة والتي قد فتحت أمامنا بابا جديدا في مجال الفكر والدعوة إلى الله معترفا بجميل الثناء على خطابكم البليغ ذومغزي تربوي فجزاكم الله خيرا على تخصيص وقت لصالح طلبتنا خلال مشاغلكم المتراكمة ونأمل أن تمنحوا لنا فرصة أخرى ولوقت كاف الإستفادة من نصائحكم وتوجيهاتكم الرشيدة .

ندعو الله سبحانه وعزوجل أن يتقبل من مساعيكم المباركة وحرصكم الشديد لصالح الأمة وهو ولي التوفيق .

مع فائق الإحترام والتقدير ،،،
والسلام عليكم ورحمة الله وبركاته ،،،

أخوكم في الله

كاكا سعيد أحمد العمري
الأمين العام للجامعة

English
Letters of Support

STANFORD
UNIVERSITY

RABBI PATRICIA KARLIN-NEUMANN
*Senior Associate Dean for
Religious Life*

Omer Salem
Managing Director
The International Organization for Peace
PO Box 1218
Palo Alto, CA 94302

4 March 2009/8 Adar 5769

Dear Omer and The International Organization for Peace,

    Thank you for your initiative and the vision set out in the White Paper in creating the Solh/S'likhah/Reconciliation Project for the International Organization for Peace.

    In a world in which listening to the already converted--whether to a religion or a political position--too often takes precedence over understanding and expanding perspectives, the vision of Solh/S'likhah/Reconciliation that you have set out for the International Organization for Peace is a welcome one. I know from our work at Stanford with multi-faith dialogue in the Fellowship for Religious Encounter and other settings, that building trust across divides can change the way potential leaders think, feel and lead. I heartily endorse your desire to apply that capacity for listening to the Israeli-Palestinian conflict. As educator Parker Palmer has said, "You can't hate someone once you know his or her story." We know that listening leads to empathy and doing so, creates understanding. If this is true among individuals, your efforts to multiply this wisdom to communities and nations, is sorely needed.

    I particularly appreciate the business aspect of your overture, as we learn that building together crosses boundaries and uproots stereotypes. It is fitting that this initiative finds fertile soil in Palo Alto, a community that values entrepreneurial and innovative approaches to seemingly intractable problems, and one that encourages education and creativity as a means to address them.

    I wish you God/Allah Speed in the project and am pleased to see the wide variety of people and expertise that are engaged in this effort.

Best wishes for Shalom/Salaam/Peace,

Rabbi Patricia Karlin-Neumann
Senior Associate Dean for Religious Life

Office for Religious Life
Memorial Church, Stanford, CA 94305-2090 T 650.725.0010 F 650.725.7009 rabbipkn@stanford.edu

ENGLISH LETTERS OF SUPPORT

City of Palo Alto
Office of the Mayor and City Council

February 23, 2009

Omer Salem, Managing Director
International Organization for Peace
P.O. Box 1218
Palo Alto, CA, 94302

Dear Omer:

Thank you for taking the time to meet with me to discuss the International Organization for Peace (IOP). I was impressed by your vision, and wish you all the best in bringing about informal talks, input and proposals from Palestinians, Israelis, Westerners, Muslims, Jews and Christians.

Although the dialogue is just in its early stages, and there will no doubt be many difficulties to overcome in the years ahead, this promises to be a breakthrough in the long struggle to achieve a lasting solution to the Israel-Palestine conflict. Thanks to the efforts you and the Commission have made in facilitating informal dialogue, formal talks are more likely to take placed between Israeli and Palestinian leaders.

May your efforts be crowned with success. and may the prayers of all who desire peace, especially those who have suffered war and repression for so many years, be finally answered.

Be assured that I will continue to support you and the IOP peace projects. If I can be of any assistance to you, please don't hesitate to let me know,

With sentiments of deep respect and admirations, I wish you all the best.

Sincerely,

Peter Drekmeier

Peter Drekmeier
Mayor

P.O. Box 10250
Palo Alto, CA 94303
650.329.2477
650.328.3631 fax

THE MISSING PEACE

The Church of the Nativity

March 25, 2009

Mr. Omer Salem, Managing Director
International Organization for Peace
380 Hamilton Ave., #1218
Palo Alto, CA 94301

Dear Omer,

    I was very pleased to be able to speak with you about IOP and the very admirable goals it has of bringing about peace and reconciliation among all the people of the Holy Land. It is certainly the fervent hope and prayer of all people of good will and faith to wish that true and lasting peace can be established among the people who share belief in the One God.

    I admire you commitment to this wonderful goal and wish you much success in your efforts. As, yourself a man of faith, you know that real peace is God's gift to us. We must work to make that gift a reality to the benefit of all. Prayer is one of the most important means of achieving this peace. All other efforts: education, communication, cultural awareness, etc. can bear fruit if in accord with God's will.

    I especially admire your emphasis on reconciliation and forgiveness. I believe these efforts, carried out with transparency and frankness on a personal level will bring about change. The many years of violence and astringency have produced nothing toward a culture of justice and peace. Non-violent understanding is the only secure path for people of reason and faith.

    Please know that my prayers accompany you on your upcoming trip to the Holy Land.

Sincerely,

Steven Otellini

Msgr. Steven D. Otellini
Pastor

210 Oak Grove Avenue
Menlo Park, CA 94025-3218

www.nativitymenlo.org

tel 650-323-7914
fax 650-323-3231

ENGLISH LETTERS OF SUPPORT

בס"ד

Congregation Emek Beracha
4102 El Camino Real
Palo Alto, CA 94306

(650) 857-1800 (v)
(650) 857-0601 (f)

Rabbi Yitzchok Feldman
(650) 857-1800
rabbi@emekberacha.org

Office
(650) 857-1800
info@emekberacha.org

Board of Directors

Aron Rosenfeld
President
(650) 565-0089
ar@emekberacha.org

Eli Schwartz
Vice President
es@emekberacha.org

Nina Brody
Treasurer
treasurer@emekberacha.org

Guy Wilnai
Secretary
gw@emekberacha.org

Laurence Marton
Past President
(650) 494-1818
lm@emekberacha.org

Rabbi Avrohom Apt
Director
aa@emekberacha.org

Phil Deutsch
Director
pd@emekberacha.org

Benjie Flusberg
Director
bf@emekberacha.org

Michal Lev Ram
Director
mv@emekberacha.org

Josh Pincus
Director
jp@emekberacha.org

Presidents' Council
Yasha Gofman
Eliot Klugman
Stan Sussman
Judith Wallach

web: www.emekberacha.org
info: info@emekberacha.org
ebb: ebb@emekberacha.org

March 4, 2010

To Whom It May Concern,

In every era, there are inviduals and groups that are willing to play the role of *Avram Halvri*, Abram the One Who Crossed (to the Other Side). This is a reference to the Torah's use of this phrase in Genesis, 14:13, when Our Father Avraham was sought out to save his nephew Lot from captivity. He is referred to by this name here because it denotes one who is willing to dwell on one side of the river even while all of the great personages and institutions of the day are arrayed on the other side. It is to such a man of fortitude and faith that one looks when one needs a daring and difficult deed.

One such organization willing to play that lonely role is the International Organization for Peace (IOP). For a few years now, it has sought a just and peaceful solution to the insoluble conflict between Israel and its Arab neighbors. By working persistently and patiently with all sides of the conflict, and by insisting that there must be a non-violent way to express differences, the organization is unique and welcome in its attempt to mediate some kind of a solution to the conflict.

We wish them well and hope that they find a way to prevail in this formidable endeavor.

Rabbi Yitzchok Feldman
Congregation Emek Beracha

Congregation Kol Emeth
4175 Manuela Avenue
Palo Alto, CA 94306
Voice (650) 948-7498 Fax (650) 948-2712

Sheldon Lewis, Rabbi Emeritus

March 21, 2009
26 Adar 5769

To Whom It May Concern:

I am very pleased to write on behalf of the International Organization For Peace (IOP). I have been involved in its founding meetings, and I am deeply impressed by the depth of its commitment to finding a just and peaceful solution to the Arab-Israel conflict and beyond. The effort is truly interfaith, inclusive, and open. Muslims, Jews, and Christians are among its members. Its vision is very ambitious, growing as it is from the grass-roots. I find the people involved to be completely genuine and able to listen closely to the often conflicting narratives surrounding this conflict. I am also convinced by its insistence that there are shared dreams and values beneath the many layers of pain and loss upon which a lasting solution can be found. I find inspiration also in the conviction by the founders that bedrock religious values in each of our faith traditions can support a secure and peaceful future.

I heartily support the IOP.

Cordially,

Sheldon Lewis

ENGLISH LETTERS OF SUPPORT

Omer Salem
IOP
PO Box 1218
Palo Alto, CA 94302

Dear Br. Omer

I wanted to extend to you my gratitude and that of our mosque for the extremely important and timely venture you have embarked upon.

We live in a time where most people in the word have grown extremely skeptical about any possibility of peace in the Middle East. There are some that keep perpetuating the grim notion that the Israeli-Palestinian conflict is inevitable, considering the inherent struggle between Muslims and Jews.

We certainly believe that this is utter falsehood and your efforts is a great testament that peace is not only attainable, but within reach.

As Muslim Americans, we need to understand that our presence in this great land is a privilege and a responsibility. Our government can do much more to broker honest and just peace between Palestinians and Israelis and I think your effort is setting the standards for that kind of activism in our community.

We applaud your efforts and pronounce our support to your endeavors in anyway possible.

Please let us know if there is anything we can do to help this great venture.

M. A. Azeez

Imam
Sacramento Area League of Associated Muslims
4541 College Oak Dr.
Sacramento, CA 95841
Office: (916) 979-1935
Fax: (916) 979-1002
Email: Azeez@salamcenter.org

THE MISSING PEACE
THE ROLE OF RELIGION IN THE ARAB-ISRAELI CONFLICT

INDEX

A
Abraham - ii, xii, 1, 2, 6, 7, 16, 18, 20, 22, 49, 53, 62, 73, 105, 108, 113, 123, 124
Al-Azhar - xiv, 4, 10, 27, 35, 61, 69, 90, 97, 109, 117, 120, 159
Anti-Semitism - 30, 51, 69, 70
Arab -1-8, 17, 22, 24, 26, 31, 32, 35, 36, 38, 39-55, 59, 61, 64, 69-71, 79, 80, 102, 106, 108, 110, 112, 119, 124, 126, 127
Ashkenazi - 47, 51
Assimilation - 24, 54, 55

B
Babi Yar - 48
Babylonian exile - 48
Balfour Act - 31
Barack Obama - 3, 6, 26, 129, 119, 120, 123
Berkeley - xiv, 85, 159
Bible - 4-8, 15, 16, 20, 27, 29, 31, 53, 54, 60-62, 64, 108, 117, 120, 121
Borders - 39, 40, 42, 46, 75, 124

C
Cairo - xiv, 3, 27, 28, 35, 42, 53, 57, 64, 69, 79, 120, 123
Calcutta - 123
Cape Town - 123
Capital punishment - 19
Casablanca - 123
Christianity - 1, 9, 16, 17, 19, 25, 70, 80, 105, 113
Converso - 70
Copenhagen - 123

D
David - 62, 121
Deuteronomy - 19, 33, 40, 57
Dhimmi - 55, 57, 135
Dignitism - 15, 23, 25, 70, 71, 101, 103, 104, 107, 135
Dignity - 3, 8, 50, 51, 57, 71, 103, 115, 120
Divine - 9, 10, 18, 19, 21, 106, 109, 114

E
Egypt - xiv, 2, 6, 22, 35, 39, 45, 46, 48, 56, 64, 69, 76, 109, 123, 124
Egyptian - 4, 45, 52, 124
Enemies - 9, 48, 68, 74
Evangelicals - 15
Exiles - 30
Exodus - 30, 46, 47, 48, 52

173

F
Forgiveness - 56, 71, 102
Friend - xiv, 2

G
Genesis - 7, 8, 40, 110
Germany - 48, 56

H
Haram - 62-64, 84, 85
Hasidic - 15, 33
Healing - 49, 74, 80
Hebrew - 4, 7, 8, 10, 17, 20, 22-27, 45, 53, 59, 62, 102, 108, 112, 116
Henry Truman - 119
Holocaust - 47, 48, 51
Holy Land - 4, 6-10, 17, 25, 26, 29, 30, 35-41, 43-54, 59-65, 72, 74, 76, 79, 88, 93, 106, 120, 123, 124, 126, 127, 159
Holy Sepulcher - 112

I
Ibrahim - 105, 107
India - xiv, 37, 64, 90, 102, 120
Inquisition - 48, 49
Iran - iv, 2, 6, 41, 46, 56, 64, 78
Iraq - 6, 39, 46, 49, 51, 64, 78
Isaac - 1, 62
Islam - xiv, 1-6, 15-19, 22, 24, 25, 31, 32, 38, 46, 50, 55, 61, 64, 70, 71, 73, 75, 76, 78, 79, 102, 105, 107, 109, 110, 111, 113
Ismail - 48
Israel - 1, 2, 4-8, 15, 22, 29-65, 70, 71, 74-79, 81, 82, 111, 117, 119-122, 124, 127

J
Jacob - 60, 62
Jerusalem - 26, 41, 42, 45, 55, 56, 61-64, 71, 72, 76, 77, 80, 81, 82, 84, 92, 96, 105, 112, 116, 119, 126
Jesus - 9, 23, 24, 60, 73, 80, 107, 111, 114
Jihad - 22, 127, 136
Jimmy Carter - 56
Judaism - xiv, 1, 2, 16-18, 25, 32, 40, 70, 105, 107, 108, 112, 113, 119, 136

L
Lebanon - 39-41, 122
Leviticus - 30, 82
Libya - 2, 6, 46

M
Maimonides - 19, 27
Mecca - 2, 28, 61, 62, 63, 64, 76, 105

INDEX

Mercy - 39, 42, 81, 106, 108, 109, 110, 111, 116, 117, 120
Micah - 27
Midrash - 30, 32, 33, 34
Mishna - 27
Moses - 20, 23, 24, 24, 107, 111
Moshiach - 23, 75, 77
Muhammad - 2, 20, 23, 24, 39, 44, 49, 53, 55, 59, 60, 62, 63, 64,
          71, 72, 73, 102, 104-111, 120

N
Noachide laws - 2, 5, 17-19, 25, 107, 108, 121

O
Orthodox - ii, iii, v, 15, 26, 33, 39, 48, 61, 119, 123, 136, 137

P
Palestine - 7, 8, 17, 31, 32, 35, 37, 41, 42, 43, 45, 46, 47, 48, 51, 55, 56,
         59, 60, 64, 65, 69, 76, 81, 122, 124, 126, 136, 141, 147, 151, 152
Peace - xii, 2-9
Peacemaking - 3, 4
Pentecostal - 15
Philistine - 7, 59, 60
PLO - 43, 44
Pogrom - 48
Proverb - 57, 112
Psalm - 122

Q
Quran - 10, 20, 56, 62, 63, 79, 81, 103, 111, 120, 121, 135, 136

R
Refugees - 35, 36, 37, 39, 41, 45, 45, 48, 49, 52, 74, 78, 126
Repatriation - 69, 75, 78, 79

S
Sadat - 81
Saila - 84
Saudi Arabia - 6, 28, 39, 46, 64, 81, 82, 109, 122, 127
Sephardic - 27, 44, 47, 51, 55
Settlements - 36, 38, 127
Sharia - 17, 25, 37, 52, 75, 115, 119, 135, 137
Shia - 9
Stanford - ii, xiv, 75, 82, 155, 156, 159
Sunni - 9, 137
Syria - 6, 39, 46, 76

T
Talmud - 19, 20, 28, 32, 33, 112
Temple Mount - 62, 63, 76, 77, 79, 82

175

Ten Commandments - 18
Terrorism - 38
Terrorist - 38, 38
Three oaths - 30, 32, 33
Torah - v, 4, 23, 24, 27, 29, 31, 32, 34, 40, 41, 43, 59, 70, 74, 75, 106
Tunisia - 2

U
United Nations - 32, 45, 55
United States - 1, 3, 4, 5, 6, 26, 38, 39, 62, 117, 119

Y
Yale - iv, xiv, 4, 6, 10, 22, 28, 56, 81, 91, 117, 159
Yom Kippur - 48, 52, 56, 112

Z
Zionism - 34, 40, 42, 53, 56, 76, 117, 137

THE MISSING PEACE

THE ROLE OF RELIGION IN THE **ARAB-ISRAELI** CONFLICT

THE MISSING PEACE

THE ROLE OF RELIGION IN THE **ARAB-ISRAELI** CONFLICT

About the Author

Omer Salem is a Senior Fellow of the Foundation of Religious Diplomacy, New York City, and is founder of the **Ibn Rushd Institute for Dialogue** based in Egypt and the USA, an inter-religious research association. Dr. Salem promotes the importance of using Islamic moral values as the basis for conflict resolution. He has been invited to various churches, synagogues, mosques and international conferences, where he has spoken before audiences that included members of the U.S. Senate in Washington, D.C. and members of the Israeli Knesset in Jerusalem. Dr. Salem is an honorary member of the Worldwide Association of al-Azhar Graduates. He is a candidate for PhD in Islamic Studies from the multi-university Graduate Theological Foundation and Al Azhar University in Cairo, he holds a Master's Degree from the Yale University Divinity School, and a Bachelor of Science Degree from the University of California at Berkeley.

Omer, an American-Sunni Muslim, was born in Egypt, established a career in engineering, real estate and investment in California's Silicon Valley, and is a frequent preacher among the New Haven, Connecticut Muslim community. In California he assembled a group of representatives of various faith communities across the USA and the Middle East to consider options for peace in the Holy Land based on Islamic moral values. The group produced a related white paper that is the basis of the Mellata Ibrahim ("MI") Initiative that has gained support from various religious and civil society organizations, as well as representatives from Stanford University.

Omer currently lives with his wife and children in New Haven, Connecticut USA.

A

www.ingramcontent.com/pod-product-compliance
Lightning Source LLC
Chambersburg PA
CBHW050536300426
44113CB00012B/2128